Jesus and Baseball

Jesus and Baseball

Lessons Learned About the Kingdom of God

Rodney A Drury

Editors: Gordon Roskamp, Annice Webb, Shirley Drury

Cover Work by Debbie Miller

Printed in the United States of America

Drury, Rodney A.

Jesus and Baseball: Lessons Learned About the Kingdom of God

First Edition

ISBN - – 978-1-942421-00-9

I dedicate this book to the hundreds of people who have encouraged me and supported my efforts to communicate the Kingdom of God to our generation.

Of these, my wife, Shirley Drury, has been my trusted friend, steadfast encourager and insightful assistant. What a blessing it is to be loved in practical ways.

Table of Contents

Acknowledgements

Acknowledgements

The Christian Center

When I arrived in Peoria, IL a few decades ago, there was a sports ministry where Christians could grow and people could find Jesus Christ. My family has enjoyed their service through bowling, softball, baseball and soccer. The Christian Center has been a place where we have enjoyed life and the Lord together.

I started coaching at The Christian Center to help out. I have been greatly blessed by all that I have learned and enjoyed by being associated with them.

If you live near the Peoria area and would like a great place to have fun, enjoy life and be encouraged in Jesus Christ, I think The Christian Center will help you out.

Online at: http://www.thechristiancenter.cc

The Christian Center
4100 N. Brandywine Dr.
Peoria, IL 61614
(309) 685-4218

Friends and Family

I'm a long way from that two room school house in South Dakota where I sat humiliated and bleeding after failing a spelling test. I would never have guessed that a fourth grader who learned to hate spelling and English would end up speaking and writing. My high school years of welding and electronic technology still come in handy, but I sure wish I had taken some English.

Making up for what I do not have is a long line of friends, family and encouragers. My wife, Shirley, is leading this band of supporters as she has believed in me more than I have. Thanks to all for your help and assistance.

Add to this crowd, Gordon Roskamp who edited the early draft of this book and Annice Webb, beloved mother-in-law, who spent hours finishing off the touches and giving me the confidence to write and let her fix it.

Thanks to so many for your kind words and support.

Ken Brooke

Ken Brooke is a coach that The Christian Center brought in to help coaches develop an age appropriate coaching plan and proper skill development techniques. Ken's help, over the years, gave me insight into helpful and proven methods. Many of the methods I use in practice come directly from Ken and his advice.

Ken has a history in playing and coaching and all who need a little help would be advanced by His insights. Here is his bio from the Christian Center.

Coach Brooke played college baseball and years of semi-pro ball. He coached at the HS and college levels and has been studying the MLB swing pattern and giving swing video analysis since 2005. He has worked side by side with MLB hitting coaches Ty Van Bukleo (Indians) and Brook Jacoby (Reds). He has discussed hitting mechanics with Jim Thome, Lance Berkma, Dante Bicette (Rookies hitting coach) and other professional coaches and players. Recently, he presented, "Unlocking the Secrets of MLB Swing Pattern," to an adult instructional camp in Arizona that included 14 major league (or former MLB) coaches.

Coach Brooke can be reached at

1302 W Pioneer Parkway, Peoria, IL 61615

309-678-6116

kenbrooke7@gmail.com

http://www.kenbrookehitting.com/

1 Preface

Over thirty years ago I started integrating sports and spiritual life. These lessons were mostly personal, but as my children began playing sports, I started coaching and helping with their teams. Taking on this added pleasure and responsibility started a process of gaining more insight into the Kingdom of God and how authentic love flows even in daily life and in sporting events. It has been a wonderful and exciting journey.

At the end of two decades of coaching, I put together some of these insights and started using them in teaching. The response was encouraging as people connected to the stories and spiritual applications. I hope that you will do the same.

Names have been changed. In some cases where identity might be gained through the context of the original story, I changed the context as much as possible to keep personal stories and identities hidden. I have truly enjoyed every team and every season.

2 Can't Catch

Maybe you have seen it, a coach yelling again and again at a player to "catch the ball." I have been embarrassed by being on the practice field or in a game when a coach shames a player over not catching the ball. At the Rookie level (6-8 year olds), many of these youngsters have never played baseball. For some, it is the first time they have ever played catch. Only a few begin the season with the skill to catch a pop fly or a hard-hit grounder. Most are timid, unsure of what to do and how to do it. Will yelling at them help develop their skill? Does pressuring them to do better help them?

I have seen the same thing in church life. "Pray more"; "read the Bible"; "fast" or "serve others" are common verbal commands we give in sermons or teaching. We give a shout over the crowd and assume people's skills will improve just because we told them to do better. I have been on both sides of the pulpit and know that encouragement is essential. "You can do it" is different from "do it." Actually, equipping the saints for the work of ministry involves disciplines, practices and historical ways of living.

Honestly, for the first few years I coached at this young level, I did not know what to do to help the kids improve. So we played a lot of catch because I thought practice makes perfect. What I did not realize was that basically I had no teaching ability; I assumed that each child would catch on based on experience and repetition. And yes, while I was the coach, I was not coaching. Later, through receiving some training on how to coach and research, I came up with the following plan. It seems a little "childish" at first, but the end result is worth the simple start. Confidence can be gained quickly and children find that it is much more fun to actually catch the ball.

Here is where I usually start.

Take off your glove and use the hand that you do not throw with to catch.

Toss the ball underhand one to another about three feet apart.

Lob the ball gently toward the face of the other player.

Try and catch the ball with your fingers.

Once you have the ball in your fingers, cover the ball with you other hand.

Advance from this basic toss to grounders and pop fly balls.

Later, when you put the glove back on try the following: wait as long as possible to lift your glove hand when catching a pop fly. If you don't, the children will raise their hands early and block their vision of the ball. They tend to wait until the ball is just about ready to hit them before moving their hand to see where the ball is. The result of early hand raising is often caused by the fear of getting hit in the face with the ball. Be careful not to teach "getting hit in the face." Usually, if the kids can see the ball, they will get their hand up in time.

There is also a great need in spiritual life for practical training, too. Weekly, we hear ideas and calls to impact our world. We are in desperate need of people who can walk with us through the process of development in prayer lives, forgiveness, Bible study methods and numerous other basic disciplines. I long for the day to come when we no longer shame people by endless cries to "do better", "try harder" or "be more passionate" only to have them leave our gatherings more discouraged than when they came. I truly believe that for the most part the people who are seeking the Lord are sincere, dedicated, and longing to know how to leave behind the ways of the world and walk the way of the Lord.

I also believe that every kid dreams of running and diving to make a great catch. Often, at the very first practice of the season, the kids will call for a toss that they can run and dive for. Once one child does this, most of the others will desire to "give it a try." This will be true even for the young beginner who struggles to catch a ball underhand when he is standing only three feet from you. We are people who love the exciting, the extreme, and the radical. Labeling our trainings as "basic," "fundamental" or "essential" have been replaced with the much more emotional and dynamic calls to be "radical", "awesome" and "major." I believe that until we discover the joy and love of learning, we will continue to label our events and programs with excessive titles while neglecting the foundational and basic principles. My prayer is that God will raise up some coaches who are content to "go slow" and in time excel beyond all the fast pace and "no fundamentals needed" approaches.

I recall a child who really, really wanted to be able to catch the ball. However, his desire could not make up for his lack of ability. His basic motor skills and technique of catching were not yet in place . But his desire compelled him beyond the laughter and public humiliation that often came with many of his attempts. Over and over again he resisted going back to what he considered the "baby toss," the bare handed games we played to develop basic skills. Even while other kids were having fun and enjoying this simple level of catch, he refused to take off his glove and join in. Somehow being able to perform great catches was seen as being able to attain by desire and not by training. Do we as adults too think our desires can replace our basic training?

Often I leave church gatherings grieving for those who have just undergone a radical call to be more "sold out for God and to passionately serve Him. I encounter young adults and teens who are banking on their "desires" to be enough to gain maturity and development. Many people think that if "I desire something enough, it will happen." I think we have to work and learn to fulfill our dreams and desires. I like the steps below.

Let's promote, encourage and honor the basics.

- Pick up the balls of patience and forgiveness, and remembering no wrong suffered, let's toss them around until we can master them.

- Learn to love doing the small and simple things. See yourself as significant because you enjoy God, not based on outward appearance.

- Celebrate, enjoy and be encouraged over living well every day, the basics. Don't let the "great thing you will do one day" cause you to lose sight of the great things you do every day.

- As you develop, expect to get hit in the face a few times as you develop new skills and advance in more difficult "catches."

3 Practice Getting Hit by Pitch

Since the kids on my baseball team are six to eight years old, many of the moms hang out during practice. On the day I announce that we are going to practice getting hit by a pitch, I brace myself for the first reaction. I know it sounds harmful to practice getting hit by a pitch, but not practicing this would be even more harmful.

Rookie baseball is coach pitch, so I am the one pitching for each child. Even though I try to give each batter the perfect pitch for them to hit, I know that sooner or later I am going to have an error and hit one of them. I also throw hard because I believe the flatter flying ball is easier to hit than the softball type lob, and when you do hit the faster moving ball, it goes further in the field. A kid who has hit a few slow pitches that dribble around the home plate will usually ask me to pick up the pace so that they can whack the ball out of the infield like the other kids.

So, one at a time, usually beginning with wiffle balls (plastic balls), I throw at the kids in the batter's box and have them learn the skills of turning their head and back. Little by little, I increase the speed of the pitch and the closeness to their heads. Before the first game, I would like every batter to have enough practice to avoid freezing up if a pitch comes at them.

The other side of this practice is that we, as a team, get to work out in private how to deal with a mistake. In the past, if I did not go through this development, a child would wonder if "I was mad at him," "what they did wrong," or even break down in tears as they went through the public shame of being hit "by their coach." Going through "getting hit by the pitch" practice gives them time to understand that even though I am for them, I can make a mistake that hurts them. Issues of rejection, fear and being publically humiliated can be dealt with. In our league, even if they get hit by the pitch, they do not get to go to first base. There is no reward for bad pitches.

In the spiritual community, there are a lot of assumptions that our leaders are never going to make a bad toss and if they do, it will never be in public. This is just not true. There is no need for us to go through the public rejection, insecurity and humiliation that we often experience when we fail to deal rightly with one another. Why do we tend to act as though we are "better than we are"? In posturing ourselves this way, we tend to avoid the practice of dealing with our weaknesses and faults. In most spiritual cultures that I have experienced, we justify the public failures and faults of our leaders rather than dealing honestly with them. When the hurt is severe enough, we find it easier to allow people to leave our circles of fellowship, even when they are harmed, rather than develop relationships that prepare for a public situation involving misspeaks and misdeeds.

Usually, I hit one child a year. One season, however, I hit the same kid twice in the same game. I loved this young ball player, and I knew that even though we practiced for this mistake, he was a little shaken and was going to be timid in the batter's box. His swing was going to be more protective than aggressive. I took myself out of the game and let my son, who was helping me coach at the time, pitch. It was a great way to say to him and others publically, I was wrong and you matter. I wanted to do more than "say" he mattered. I wanted to show him he mattered and that even the most powerful person on the team (the coach) is willing to make him feel valued.

Have you ever been a part of a church culture that says "I was wrong...but." "I was wrong but ...in some way it was your fault." That is not the way of Christ Jesus who humbled himself to the point of death on the cross. Giving up our positions, our status, our pride are very small things to do in loving others, and if we practice good relationships, we will find joy in the giving. Giving is not always easy. Providing a way to have lasting relationship can be difficult. But, through our efforts, we can do more than yell "look out." We can establish ways to get back on track after getting hit by a pitch.

4 Fear of Failure

Most coach pitch baseball teams are composed of kids who are full of energy and adventure. They easily "give things a try" and are mostly unaware of their skill level. They pick up bats almost their own size and often try to knock the ball "out of the park" when hitting it out of the infield would be a worthy task. Their dreams are full of fun, glory and doing well.

However, every now and then a child who has learned to fear failure will come to a practice. Getting them to "try" takes effort and convincing. In some of these cases, either Mom or Dad is making them play because it will be good for them. But often they ask to sit the bench or go to the bathroom so that they can miss playing time. It makes me both sad and angry to see such young lives bound by fear. I recall one young man who constantly gazed at the ground avoiding eye contact with players and coaches. His major goal seemed to be to plop down and wait for the end of practice or the game.

Often when I talk to these kids and ask them, "what is wrong", they tell me, "I can't hit" or "I'm no good" or "I hate baseball." Their statements are often true and when it is, I tell them so. "So you can't hit, but do you want to learn to?" Pretending they can do something, when they cannot, does not help. Encouraging them to learn, grow and develop does. The question I want them to consider in their hearts is not "what is your present state" but "can you get better?"

In the Rookie league, missing a ground ball is really not a big thing. You are hidden out in the field among nine other kids who often miss the ball. When you catch the ball, everyone gives you a high five. When you bat though, it is another matter. There you are isolated, exposed for everyone to see. There, the other team and fans count your failures. While few actually cheer for the opposing team to strike out, they do wait in eager expectation for three outs so that they can have their turn. To battle against this public pressure of performance, I have noticed an increase in the attitude of "not trying" that justifies "not doing well." If I don't care, than it is OK to do poorly. If someone does confront me with my failure, I do not face my fears, I just hide behind apathy. "It doesn't matter; I wasn't trying that hard anyway" can become a way of life.

Our spiritual communities are also filled with fear masquerading as apathy. We may assume the problem is passion, lack of interest or commitment, but often it is fear. Somehow or in some way, they have learned that "they can't do it." Maybe they can't live up to the "excellent spirit" forecasted by leadership or even those around them. Maybe the culture hides imperfections and sins so that there is an appearance of things being better than they actually are. Maybe it is just the history of a belittled and wounded person coming to the surface and crying out for help.

In my equipment bag, I have some very large plastic balls about three times the size of a baseball. I have found that taking a fearful child aside and softly tossing the balls up begins a healing process. Practice time is short and important, but in the perspective of years of enjoyment gained by overcoming fear of failure, it is worth the time taken to do this. These balls tend to make a very noisy "ping" when you hit them. Often the child I have pulled aside feels more shame or guilt at first and hardly tries to hit the balls at all. I often just ask them to do it for me.

Then the process begins. Internally, I pray that they can hit a few of these balls. If they do, their swing gets a little more energetic and a little more joyful each time. Once the balls start to "ping", other kids start to notice the hitting and often chide in "nice one." These balls also tend to fly about twice the distance of a soft baseball and so when they are hit by even the smallest of players, the ball soars. The goal of this exercise is not to learn to hit but to learn to overcome fear with joy. When they can do what they once feared, but with joy, it's a victory. You can see it on their faces and in their body language.

If within your family or spiritual community there are people battling fear, don't neglect them or assume they are unconcerned with life and God. Take the time to relate to them, and see if they reveal their real heart condition. Come away from the field of life and work together to enjoy the very thing that rules them. Share with them the goal of enjoyment and avoid the need for total victory, excellence or high performance. Hebrews 12:2 tells us that Jesus endured the cross motivated by joy. Maybe it's time to focus a little less on success and a little more on joy.

5 Play Ball

Spring breaks forth and so does the mindset that school will soon be over. Children dream of freedom. When you ask them what they are going to do this summer, the most often repeated answer is play. This has also been my experience in coaching baseball. The children who sign up to play ball for the most part have two major goals. The first is to play. The second is to play baseball. At the opening of the season if I talk about the drills, the dedication that I want from the team, the rules I want them to learn or how I don't want them to go swimming on game days, you would think that I was threatening to set their feet on fire. There may be a few hard core athletes in the crowd of seven and eight year olds, but most of them simply want to play.

How did it come about that "serious" and "fun" got separated in life? I was raised in the generation that was told to "wipe that smile off your face" anytime humor was presented in a "serious" situation. The reality is that we often need fun to be a part of serious endeavors so that we enjoy life, gain persistence and work toward maturity. I have found that every time I find a way to have fun and develop players, they advance. Often the more fun it is, the more effort is given to the drill. Most of these children did not sign up for baseball to work, but to have fun.

The Bible also has insight and directions for delighting in the Lord, being happy and rejoicing (Ps. 37:4; 104:34; 1Pet. 1:8; Isa. 61:10). Do we believe that having fun, or enjoyment is something against God and against His ways? Why is it that so many of us "serious Christians" are also such joyless Christians? I know that I have spent far too much time defining love more in terms of duty than of delight. As I mature, however, I find following, serving and obeying the Lord more and more enjoyable. Joy has earned a place in my foundation of sacrifice and devotion. I follow Jesus for the joy of it. Sure there are hard times, but the message of the good news of Jesus Christ isn't "not fun."

Baseball among our youth is in decline in America, and so is church life. Many Americans spend only a couple of hours on Sunday morning in the pursuit of God. Often the reason is credited to busyness. In part, that is true. People are busy seeking fun and having fun. Netflix may have replaced Sunday evening services, and eating out has taken over where once we had extended times of prayer following the Sunday morning service because there tends to be so little fun in following God. Why?

It is an assumption of mine that people used to enjoy God and church more. My studies of history reveal that our forefathers had a much greater ability to enjoy God than we now have. This loss of joy seems to be tied to a value shift. As a society, we used to give more value to the happiness that can be found in loving God and others. I believe that what we value tends to relate to what we enjoy and find fun in doing. When a society enjoys God, they tend to enjoy following Him.

From time to time, I run across a drill Sergeant type coach. It is "his way or no way" and he wants 110% effort all the time. I find the same thing in much of the mass media church of today. Followers of Jesus are bombarded with calls to be "this world's greatest Christians." Extraordinary people doing extraordinary things are held in high public regard and become the poster children for normal Christian living. We are called, and at times required to be like these gifted, talented, resourceful people who are serving God with abilities, callings and platforms that most of us don't have. Thus some begin to believe that success is "being extraordinary."

Baseball is also a great place to learn to enjoy being ordinary. The most skilled and gifted baseball players in the world often fail to hit the ball two out of three times they are at bat. At any time and in every season there are only ten top ten players, never any more, only ten. So the rest of the players need to find another reason for playing, for enjoying baseball. To help kids enjoy the game and move beyond the worship of success, I have a game I play. We line up and each kid is thrown a ball to catch. However, the ball is deliberately thrown beyond their reach, so each will need to dive for the ball. Trying to reach the ball is the goal, not actually catching it. Replacing the fear of not catching the ball is the joy of attempting to. Laughter and shouts of praise are given for effort. Children who stood in fear at the pressure of catching a fly ball now run and laugh with delight simply trying to. Isn't it time for the church to go beyond over valuing success and failing to reward effort?

A society that values hard work can value the effort of people and not just their success. Prosperity can be a goal of any group of people, but when prosperity becomes the focus, the value of effort is lost to the value of affluence. The average person is devalued and the top few esteemed to be kings and rulers among us. It happens in baseball, and it happens in the church.

It is great to win baseball games, and winning is a goal; it just is not the primary goal. At the coach pitch level, having fun is the primary goal. When kids have fun playing baseball, they will most likely return the next year to play ball again. If they hate the season, next year they simply won't turn up. By having fun, we are not making their happiness the center of our lives or the center of the league. Having fun is just a primary part of what we are doing. Having fun is a part of long term commitments, on the ball field and in the body of Christ.

6 Personal Responsibility

Onto the field runs Ka-boom. That's not his real name, but that title reveals the hope and potential that Ka-boom saw in himself as a seven year old ball player. Ka-boom wanted to be a great ball player and wanted others to see him that way, too. He wanted to be a star. Ka-boom was also uncoordinated, overweight and lacking in hand-eye coordination. I loved Ka-boom, and to this day I still do. I run into Ka-boom now and then; a decade has passed since he was on my team, and he is a great young man, giving, kind, hardworking and still a little clumsy.

So, who is to blame for this lack of ability? Ka-boom was not given the gifts from God that helped him fulfill his dreams about baseball. He worked hard in practice. His efforts included pushing through the discouragement that came when he failed because of his limited ability. I know we often tell people that you can do whatever you set your mind on, but that just isn't always true.

Coach pitch baseball is brutally honest. Your coach, not an opposing pitcher, tries to pitch you the perfect ball to hit. With encouragement and patience, the batter is being tossed the best pitch possible. It is not as if the batter can blame the skill on the opposing pitcher. Your coach, friend, encourager is throwing the ball in the best possible place for your success. When you strike out, who is to blame? When you go through the season without a hit, who is to blame, who is responsible?

Seven is a great age for children to learn personal responsibility, if they haven't already. Most have not. Mistakes, faults, failures and sins can be blamed on others. People often say, "My lack of ability is not my fault." Only my success is attributed to me. Failure must have a cause other than me. To complicate this even more, we all must be responsible for things that are impossible for us to change. YES, we all need to be personally responsible for things we cannot change. Seven is a great age to begin to learn this.

Addictions are becoming labeled as the result of DNA or environmental conditions. While we do want to remove the shame of getting help, we do not want to remove the personal responsibility of getting help. Sin is the biggest addictive behavior and no one can save him, clean his own heart, renew his own mind or make him/herself into a "new creation." Yet, our inability to do that does not remove our responsibility. One of the greatest aspects of coach pitch baseball is that it lays a foundation for dealing with "being born into sin." Yes, we are all responsible for dealing with the conditions given to us.

Ka-boom went through an identity crisis. His dreams and vision of himself were visible to others, and he went through the process of seeing who he really was and what value he had through another's lens. I am glad he did not have parents and peers who lied to him, who deceived him about his ability. Deception is not kind or loving. Telling people they are better than they are may win you favor for a moment, but you lose the truth. Real encouragement doesn't need deception. Honesty is not always harsh or hateful. Speaking the truth in love is a blessing to each of us as we go through transformation from self-love to true love. Ka-boom needed to be responsible for his ability and we need to be responsible for loving and valuing people regardless of performance.

As I write, I reflect on a time when Ka-boom struck out. We had men on base and any hit would have resulted in a victorious inning. I recall walking over and patting him on the back after striking out. I believe the best words I could muster were "you tried." I also recall hearing the mocks and scoffing from other parents and fans. I do not think all of them combined would equal the desire for success that Ka-boom had. Yet, they felt free to criticize this child as if he did not care; he did! They may not have understood the results of their actions, but Ka-boom was learning to understand his. I guess more people should play coach pitch baseball.

7 Coaching

We all affect the lives of others. In this book, I want to help you see and understand some of the ways we can improve by living out the community of Christ Jesus. Parents can improve their ability to instruct and guide their children. Friends can find ways to encourage and prepare one another for life. Spiritual leaders can gain wisdom in leading and mentoring. We all can do a better job of being the people of God we are called to be.

By God's grace, I hope to go beyond illustrations and challenges to "try harder" or "be more passionate." I hope to move beyond the temptations of pressuring people with time and lofty goals. I hope that each one of us may gain an understanding of the ways of God and thus have a heart transformation that leads us into being different toward one another. I know that seems like a lofty goal, but possible.

I have seen 6, 7 and 8 year old boys be transformed in a few weeks. These young men all progressed at different levels, but all progressed. Year after year, I have been amazed that development does happen. Relationships that are Godly can also quickly bear positive fruit. When we serve one another through coaching, we give our love and insight away for God's glory and the improvement of others. As you read this book, make note of what good things you are already doing that can be enhanced and, if the Spirit convicts, what things you can stop doing. You are surrounded by people who need your friendship, your insight and at times, your coaching.

Our world is full of people focused on their own successes. In the Kingdom of God the success of one is linked to the condition of others. Jesus came to give us abundant life. Each one of us can be like Him and also help others have a better life. The "better life" may not be visible in what they do, but in who they are. Coaching often deals with changing the inside. The outside will catch up.

Join me in the quest to help others. You can use baseball or music, science or video. It doesn't matter. Take whatever skill you have and package it, present it, to help others.

8 Having Fun

"We are not here to play around and have fun, we are here to play ball." This cry, usually coming from a parent of a player, is often heard at one of our first practices of the year. Parents and people intent on playing baseball lose sight of the first word in that endeavor: "playing." I know not everyone sees it my way and there are plenty of options for finding intense, focused, demanding and performance driven teams. I simply want to opt for maturity via playing.

Why do young boys give up their summer and risk the public shame of striking out or the embarrassment of missing the ball? Do these children care more about being sound baseball players, or are they looking for some activity that produces joy and fun in their lives? I believe that they play baseball to have fun. Rookie baseball (6-8 year olds) may be seen in many different ways, but for almost all the kids I have ever coached, they want to "have fun" playing ball. No fun = no ball playing. Children who are not having fun do not want to come to the games, let alone practice. You can tell in just a few weeks which kids are there because Mom or Dad demands it, and which kids are having fun. We tend to think of "fun" as not important, lacking in dedication, with optional effort. However, what "having fun" is, is a fast track for growth and maturity.

Our Father in heaven gives commands, demands compliance to His will, and has passion and purpose for His will being accomplished on the earth. Father God seeks a relationship with His children that results in healthy, whole and wonder filled living. Is "having fun" a main motivation for us? Yes.

Over the years, I have seen that those who "enjoy God," those who "delight in God," and who "love loving God," have a more Christ-like life than those who are passionately seeking to live a life worthy of His calling based on performance. It is as if they are trying to become great at being Godly without the enjoyment and motivation of love. These can become commitment-driven people seeking to please the Father while having little or no real love for Him. People of duty, getting everything right, often really feel disconnected from God and His pleasure in them. Delighting in God is foundational. Psalms 37:4 says to delight in the Lord and He will give us the desires of our heart. Loving and enjoying God is foundational to purpose.

More and more over the last ten years, as I travel and speak, I have encountered people in the church who are mad at God. They don't say it in public, but when you talk as friends, that anger comes out. God has broken some deal with them. They have tried to earn some level of holiness, transformation or healing through fasting, Bible reading, church attendance or spiritual service and have not received the reward they wanted for their performance. They have lost a relationship with God and now live the Christian life based on a list of "do's" and "don'ts." Many have shut up their emotions toward God, choosing to focus on hanging on until the end. They avoid any desire to encounter God because their heart is wounded from years of performance- based living with little or no results. The results I am speaking of here are not the outward list of accomplishments, but the inward reality of their inner man. They find themselves able to "play the game" yet have little passion and love for God and for life.

God is holy, righteous, powerful, awesome and enjoyable. If we live in such a way as to make delighting in God, and enjoying Him a main focus of our lives, do you think we will live closer to Him? The more I enjoy being with the Lord, the more I am transformed by His grace and presence. The hope of holiness and righteousness is gained through fellowship with God, not duty-driven practice. I am not talking of cheap grace here or complacency in following Christ. Love often requires sacrifice, humility and pain. Going through the hard things of life is not proof that God doesn't care. Even in our hard places, God cares and we feel His love. We can delight in God; we can be people who whole heartedly love God for Himself and end up living the lives He desires us to live.

In baseball, almost every year, I have some kind of confrontation with a parent about having a "fun" focus over a "performance driven" focus. I have learned to just wait. I now know that if I can help this child have a love for the game, he will quickly want to learn the rules, the proper techniques and will play with passion. Fun is a big part of formation, natural and spiritual. When was the last time you grew spiritually because you felt joy in doing so? When was the last time your sense of duty was less than your excitement of enjoying God? I hope your response was, "just yesterday."

9 Swing Hard

Time spent in the batting cage is time spent developing hand-eye coordination. A child who is given three or four hundred swings tends to learn to hit. Those who struggle the most usually have a dad or coach constantly tweaking their form, adjusting their grip and turning their natural swing. The advice I got years ago in a coaching clinic and which has proved to be true is to "swing hard."

We can take what players learn to do naturally, or we can destroy that natural ability by trying to make them perform in a set way. There are sound fundamentals and proven methods for hitting, and these basic proven techniques should be practiced. Yet, even at the professional level, dealing with a player's natural ability should be considered along with the fundamentals. Most seven year olds do best when given a vast supply of encouragement and opportunity. Helping our players develop their abilities and not just to hit in a prescribed way will have results that both the player and the coach can enjoy. Using the fundamentals of good hitting, we adjust our methods to each player and help them all. We take what we know and use it to help them.

Six through eight year old boys have limited focus and "over coaching" can paralyze them. When their eyes glaze over trying to process all the instructions they have been given, it is time for a break. It is time to ask them to take a deep breath and swing hard. Most of us find it easier to focus on one thing at a time.

We also need to be careful about demanding conformity to a method. Boundaries are good and necessary but a "one size fits all" approach to life and ministry is not the Jesus way. Rules and methods are often established for two reasons. The first is that we are trying to protect people. Maybe we have seen people get hurt in the past, so we develop rules to protect them. The second is that we are trying to have control. By controlling others, or trying to, we fulfill the pressure we have "to lead" or to "coach." Standardization helps with boundaries and control. Unfortunately, many times we tend to end up focusing on the rules and lose sight of people.

Among the people of God, the real prize is loving God, loving others, and doing our part in the Kingdom. This is my summary of the first two great commands and the Great Commission which I believe are foundational. Attempting to build on this foundation, or any other, we can develop a "how we are going to do this" method that in time becomes more important than our initial goals. Our vision drifts away from the foundation as we respond to increased pressure to do things in the right method, "the right way." Our views of self and service can become very judgmental when "doing it this way" is seen as the only right way. Love for God and others can fade as we continue to pressure and coach everyone into our methods. Having everyone on the same page, using the same methods and speaking the same words may appear as unity and harmony, but it can be deceiving. Conforming to the image of Jesus Christ requires personal diversity. Hitting the ball is a combination of being who you were made to be and the integration of the fundamentals.

My spiritual community includes artists, musicians, nurses, doctors, bus drivers, teachers, engineers, film makers, authors and a variety of other occupations and endeavors. The items we bring to a pot luck meal show our diversity as we find the organic and all natural next to the fried chicken and processed snacks. On Sunday, you may find the worship team is a string quartet, the next, a keyboard playing contemporary music, and on the third a throwback to the sixties with hymns and choruses. While we all have our preferred music, we also should practice the principle of "swinging hard." We try to encourage one another to be who God made them to be. Loving one another from the heart includes a desire that each person uniquely express him or herself. Cheering others on is a way to shift our emotions away from "what we like" toward loving others in a way that is encouraging to them.

Discipleship is an important part of following the Lord. When conformity to information or to a method is the rule, we fail. We succeed by helping coach and assist people into being conformed into the image of Christ Jesus. This success is a reproduction of the heart of Jesus, a transformation just as in coach pitch baseball, we can see this transformation when a child steps up to the plate with confidence that he is going to hit the ball. It may not always happen, but the player has confidence that it will. In spiritual community, we can see this transformation when people have this same confidence in following the Lord. They may not get everything right, but their hearts are set on Him and they are going to give it all they have as they swing hard for His glory. With freedom, we can learn to swing hard even as we continue to mature. The balance between the fundamentals and personal expression will get worked out as we continue to practice the faith and baseball.

10 Rules

I grew up in a world of rules. It was a "one size fits all" world. In my family, every member was to comply, no exceptions. So later in life when I met my wife, who comes from the world of relationships, I entered into a strange and new field. She did not make decisions based on rules, but on relationships. Her world was strange and unusual. I co-existed in this world for many years, and then I started coaching children in baseball. That was when I began to go beyond co-existing and enter into the world of relationships.

When I first began coaching, I also had a bunch of rules that helped me manage the team. I had rules for being in the dugout, rules for cleaning up, rules for letting me know about attendance, rules for about everything. Over time, I found myself not relating to the kids; I was there to coach, but I actually became just the "rule enforcer." I protected myself from trouble by having rules. I avoided dealing with a child personally by referring him to the rules and informing him "that's the way it is" and that he needed to follow the rules. I had no need to connect to a child; I did not need to understand them or what they thought; I just needed them to follow the rules, and we would have a great season.

It all began to change the day a father brought me his son to play on the team. This potential player had no glove, was wearing dress shoes and had slacks on. This boy had never played and wanted to be a part of the team, and had no idea about the game or "my rules." I found myself taking the time to get him the equipment needed and to talk to him about how the game is played. We had long conversations about the team and how he could fit in. I started using a diagram for the positions so players could find their position from a picture on a clip board hanging in the dugout. Now players did not need to embarrass themselves by publically asking where right field or short stop was.

That was the year I learned to relate more, and rule less. Sure the rules made my life easier, because I didn't need to explain so much and so often. The rules helped me get things done without needing a good reason. The players had no need to understand the reason. They just needed to follow the rules. This was the year that also helped me see how many things I was doing for me and not for the team. I have not become an anti-rule guy, but I came to see how I was using rules instead of relationships. You could say I was controlling.

The rule for sitting on the bench and in their batting order was a good rule for me, and it helped speed up the game as each player knew who was next at bat. But, it also did little to help young boys learn to deal with energy and emotions. It reduced the joy of playing - a lot. Joy was now found only in batting or playing the field. The dugout felt more like detention. The rule of keeping each player's hat and glove together was also a great rule to help me manage the team, and removing this rule led to throwing gloves and losing hats. We had hats on wrong players and hats in the dirt. At first the "throwing hat in the dirt" thing seemed bad, but some boys like dirt and dust. In time, each team learns which players are "neat and clean" and which players take the time to jump in mud puddles. Rules control chaos, but they limit fun.

Coaching is more work now. Coaching now requires that I talk to individuals, that I work out personal issues, and that I help team members find boundaries. I have found that I am there for the kids.

Life in the church can also have a lot of rules. Most of these, I am afraid, are for the same reasons I used rules in coaching, to control people. When we "over rule" we do little about making disciples, but train people to simply comply and not to be transformed. We project the attitude that attending our church requires following the rules, and if they do not, they are not welcome. Even if people must pretend to comply, we don't care. Just follow our rules.

Sadly, we are not consistent even in our rules. We break the rules for friends or under pressure. We have hundreds of rules for other people, but not for the leaders' family, or the generous givers, or the power controllers. We assume that in church life we are too busy to relate to each one personally. We often have a mindset of a business and not of family. The cost of having a "rules run" spiritual community is overwhelming. Literally half of those who love God hate His church. That's the statistic now; half of those who say they love Jesus don't want anything to do with church. Yes, we need standards and policy, but we must also need relationships. Relationships are the first and second great commands of the Lord. Sending someone a memo regarding a policy is not the same as talking to them over coffee. If you don't have the time for people, only time to enforce the rules, maybe you don't have time to coach. Maybe you have built a team that is more about you than about them? This applies to families, small groups, home groups and most any time we have people in relationships. Success is not just getting a job done, but it is also how we got the job done and who was helped along the way.

What is it that really drives us? Do we love God and others or are we accomplishing some task, program or agenda item? We must keep the first things first. Do we think people will be lifelong followers of Jesus based on following rules or based on following the person of Jesus? How many of us recall the lessons taught us in Sunday School? How many of us recall the love and care of the person teaching those lessons? Relationships matter.

By the end of that summer of unlearning, I had changed. I had more issues than ever before, but I also had closer relationships with the players and their families. The task that I was given to accomplish, coaching rookie baseball, was still accomplished. We learned how to get out of the dugout quickly and how to clean up. But we also learned how to do these things via relationships, not rules. Order had become less important than smiles. Look for churches where everybody smiles.

11 Playing To Win

In our coach pitch league a base runner cannot take an extra base on an overthrow. This rule allows the players to try to make plays and avoid being penalized for that attempt. For example, one day we were in a close game. Emotions were high and both teams were in the hunt for a win. We had a player on third when a ball was hit somewhere in the infield and the throw made to first. The young man on third did not attempt to run home, because according to the rules, he was required to remain on third. But when the throw at first went wild, we coached him to run home and thus score the winning run. We won the game, but at what cost?

In the excitement, few people knew what actually happened. The other team and their coaches did not pick up on the violation, or if they did, they let it go. One young man in our dugout noticed the violation and just looked at me. To my regret, I just looked at him and said, "We won."

From my years of coaching and playing sports, I have perceived two types of "playing to win." The first type is "do your very best, stay focused, be fully committed." The second type is to "do whatever it takes to win." "Doing whatever it takes to win" is evil. I use "evil" because Scripture used that word to describe what our present days are filled with.

The day I cheated, the worst evil that I committed was not the violation to win the game. The real evil was the seeds I sowed in the hearts of my team. I mentored them in the wicked thought that there are areas of our lives where the rules and values of the Kingdom of God do not apply. I invested in separating ourselves from God based on what we are doing. Cheating because it is only a game will one day lead to cheating to win at work, cheating to get what you want from your family and cheating to make yourself happy in life. Helping people get there is wicked and evil indeed... and so is a "winning at all cost" mindset.

In family life, work and church, the "win at all cost" attitude sets us up to appear as Godly, but inwardly be filled with evil. We can pursue Godly ends with ungodly means. Patience, kindness, not remembering a wrong suffered, or simple generosities are all avoided so that we can achieve a result. If we are not careful (full of care), we can deceive ourselves that what we do is more important than how we do it. A quick review of 1 Cor. 13 should readjust that mindset.

Jesus knew what He came to do and walked out His calling, continually dealing with other people. He knew when He had to isolate himself and when He had to travel at night so that His purpose could be fulfilled. In all His ways, Jesus did not seek to win at all cost, but kept on surrendering Himself to the Father. God the Father was co-responsible for the outcome. Jesus was to hear and obey. We may often feel like what we do is all up to us. God has promised us that He would not leave us or forsake us. The Holy Spirit is ever with us, so we must battle the pressure to do things in our own strength. For it is this, "I got to get this done somehow" that leads to compromising, cutting corners and cheating. While we serve with all our hearts, we know that unless the Lord helps us, victory is not possible. A focus that values "how something is done" more than the results will help us live on a solid foundation.

Sports are such a strong cultural power in America that we need to work hard to see through some of the negative influences they bring. Sports are also filled with opportunities for discipline and life lessons. Focus, team work, sacrifice, honor and humility are a few of the positives that playing sports can produce in our lives. A pitfall is determining value based on the results of a competitive event, winning or losing. "Winners" may be people who win in our culture, but Christians are people who transcend winning and offer to our world a much wider and deeper understanding of life, worth and value. Setting the bar at winning is setting the bar too low.

Often I remember that game. I wish I had the opportunity to redo the ending play. I wish that I had the opportunity to respond to the probing eyes of the youth I brushed off under the emotions of winning a game. Those events are past now. Yet, similar situations will arise again, and I hope that when they do I will choose wisdom over winning.

12 False Praise

Love is patient; love is kind; love does not remember a wrong suffered, and love does not lie.

From time to time, you will get a player on the team who is being over encouraged. Often, it is a child who has very low motivation and encouragement is given to keep him going and built up. Someone tries to over complement in order to get his emotions back to normal. At other times, the player is highly motivated and the encouragement is given more as praise, esteem. This can turn into a "you can do no wrong" situation, and this situation is often encouraged by either the giver or receiver. For me, "over encouragement" occurs when it becomes false praise.

Saying to a child, who seldom gets a hit, "you are one of the best players on the team" or saying to the child who lies down in the field and pulls the grass up, "you are an amazing player" is sowing lies in the child. It is enough for a child to be who he/she is, and we love and care for each of them based on that alone. There is no need for false praise. The result of false praise is a deep wounding of the heart, not encouragement. I recall a situation where a child was playing at the pitcher position and a ball, slowly hit, rolled out toward him. He walked over and picked up the ball with his bare hand. Praise from an excited parent erupted, "that's awesome, great catch." It was a moment when false praise seemed more like mocking than encouragement.

One situation of false praise involved a mom who was a real encourager. After her son struck out or froze up after picking up a grounder, she would walk behind our dugout and tell him that he was a great player, that he was one of the best. A few times when we needed a hit and he was up to bat, I recall the verbal encouragement and praise of how great he was. I can also recall the conversations on the bench when he told me "my Mom lies" and "I suck."

False praise brought to this child and to all others who live under the umbrella of false praise is an ongoing dark cloud of deception. False praise causes people to live under a lie. False praise is not encouragement; it is rejection hidden beneath kind words, failure masked by an inability to speak the truth in love. In the end, if it is not corrected, children can end up living a lie of who they are, never dealing with reality, but living a fantasy.

As a coach, I frequently dealt with boys who want to play ball but have little skill. Often they start fishing in our conversations to draw praise from me. Over the last few years, I have experienced more and more pressure by the players not to just tell them they are doing a "good job" or that was a "nice catch," but to give them extraordinary high praise in every word I say. All the seeds we have sown in our society about being radical, awesome, magnificent, outstanding and glorious are now coming to maturity. Many now see average as failure. Hard work is of no reward unless it produces outstanding results.

The truth is that most of us are average. If we were all so "wonderful", then wonderful would be the new average. We simply need to break our addiction to be the best and help one another enjoy who we are. We need to stop lying to our children and simply love them. I often respond to the "I suck" comments in the dugout with "so - are you having fun?" If we only enjoy doing what we are "the greatest at", most of us are going to have a very joyless life.

False praise has also worked its way into the Christian community as well, and we have a mass of people who live in deception. Have you ever sat through a lesson taught by someone who cannot teach? After the lesson, people who were bored to death praised the instructor, thinking they were being Christian rather than seeing themselves as lying? Maybe you have heard someone sing, or make a budget report or run the sound system with the action being bad but the praise being good. How is lying to these people helping them? Are we not in reality causing them to undergo years of hidden shame? Are we not despising them, causing them to think more highly of themselves than they ought to while others gossip and talk negatively about them behind their back?

On the ball field, I try to speak the truth in love. When confronted by players who are bad, I tell them they can't play very well, but that if they practice and work hard, they will get better. I also tell them that I like them no matter how great or how badly they play. I want them to know our relationship and my care for them is not based on their performance, but simply upon who they are.

In the end, removing false praise allows us to truly celebrate when something good is done. For example, on one occasion, a child was playing third base when a line drive ball was hit extremely hard for his age level. In a mixture of self defense and what he had learned through practice, he instinctively stuck the glove in front of his body and caught the line drive. Everyone wowed in wonder and praise. The wonder of that moment could sink in deep because it was real. He had done something amazing, and he didn't need false praise to make the deed valuable. Life will provide enough opportunity for real praise; we do not need the false. If we withhold the false, the real will be able to do its job well enough.

13 Mistakes

Mistakes are a part of learning. This may seem like a basic truth but there are many who feel they should already know how to do everything they attempt to do. All too often when we start to teach a player how to play, they cower in shame, or boast, "I know how to do it." Onto the field trots a six year old player who has never batted; should he know how to bat? A seven year old player, who has never played shortstop runs across the field and into position; should he know how to field that position? For some reason, children in our culture are reacting to a pressure that they should already know how to do something, even if they have never done it.

Maybe the source of this internal pressure is how we treat one another. Every now and then a dad will yell at a child, "don't you know how to _____." We are a busy people, and in our rush we often forget that teaching, instructing, and training are needed. In my attempts to get the team ready for game day, I too, can lose sight of the reality that personal instruction is needed. My attitude can foster the need to appear to know how to perform. It takes time to learn, and our children are reacting to a world that is often too busy for mistakes. The joy of learning and practice can be lost in the frustration of not already knowing how to.

I know that sounds basic, so let me put it in real life situations. Timothy is playing second base with a runner on first. The ball is hit to him near second base, and all he needs to do is pick up the ball and step on second. Instead, he tries to make the throw to first and is unsuccessful. Now we have runners on second and third. Timothy is coached that when "that" happens all he needs to do is touch second. The very next batter hits the ball in the same place. Timothy proudly grabs the ball and steps on second. There was not a runner on first to cause a forced out, so Timothy should have made the play to first. When Timothy did that just one play prior, that was the wrong choice. Now as life would have it, the very next player hits the ball to second again and Timothy aggressively fields the ball. In an attempt not to make any mistakes, he simply holds onto the ball and waits for someone to tell him what to do. I know this situation seems abnormal, but actually, I have lived it out over and over and over again on the ball field.

Failure to coach in such a way as to provide space for mistakes results in frustration. Anxiety and stress will dominate the lives of the players if they cannot make mistakes. How many people do not have a love for learning because they are afraid to make a mistake? Fear and worry will actually cause players to be paralyzed and the joy of playing a game will be lost. So how do we handle mistakes?

There is not a "one size fits all" formula for dealing with mistakes. In life, some failures result in the loss of life, while some just result in a runner advancing to third. I want to deal with the "little mistakes," the "learning mistakes" of life. For these, we need to practice both discipline and patience. We need discipline to learn from the situation, and patience for the lesson to sink in.

As a rookie baseball coach, I was experiencing, with Timothy, the lessons of that day. My pride or desire to win, or how I thought people were judging me as coach, all came into play. I could easily lose sight of the reality that what Timothy was learning would make him a happier and better player years from now. I could pressure him "in the moment" and fail to see how learning works. I could demand performance which is different from encouraging it.

Often in the context of repeated mistakes, I need to loudly announce, "Everything is OK." By informing the team that I am not mad and that we have no need to panic helps keep panic and anger from sweeping the field. Often, if I step forward and yell out to Timothy "that's my fault, Tim, I should have told you what to do," the whole atmosphere of failure is turned to hope. Because a child is not left alone, he doesn't feel the pressure to succeed on his own. Helping cover mistakes helps in learning.

Sins, faults and failures in the life of a Christian are often hidden away or blown out of proportion. Few church meetings have time at the altar where someone can go, repent, and get a fresh start on life. Most of us must deal with our repentance in private, away from the atmosphere of corporate forgiveness and embrace. Often the way we deal with sin results more in our identity than in learning experiences. We know that we should not make such mistakes, but who is there to help us? We lack spiritual coaches who can help us grow. We have more than enough "fans" to comment and criticize. Mistakes are a part of life in Christ? We mature through errors, and maturity is not the result of error free living.

There are disciplines we can use for turning our failures into learning and maturing experiences. For now, I want to build the foundation that mistakes are a part of life and do not need to be our identity. Don't hide your mistakes, but don't promote them; don't dismiss them, but don't advertise them. Be content to learn and you will progress into a more mature person. Focus on how mature you "ought" to be, and you will most likely not advance at all. Focus on what you can learn from your failures, and you have chosen a pathway to maturity.

14 Playing in the Dirt

In rookie baseball most of the hits are in the infield. You take your turn playing the outfield where you might possibly not have a ball hit to you all year. In our league, we have four outfielders, so we have four positions every inning that can be quite boring. If a coach does not rotate the positions every inning, a player, even a focused player can end up "doing time in the outfield." When a player becomes more a prisoner than a player, you can see it. He starts kicking the dirt.   Then he will stare at the landscape, birds in flight, and dandelions in the grass. If he is not given a significant position to play, he will end up entertaining himself. In time, he will kneel down or lie down and start playing in the dirt. Roads, pathways or just piles of dirt to kick around become the resources he uses to help him get through standing in the sun for an hour.

Every player has a need to be needed. Why should he show up if he doesn't matter?   Why try to focus if the most exciting activity is picking up one ball that three other guys standing next to him can get. When we get bored, we play in the dirt.

The same thing happens in spiritual life.   People are a part of a community; they come, give their offerings, and support the staff and events.   But maybe they are just in the outfield. They may be told they are significant, but how they are treated must back that up. We can tell people all the time they matter, but if that does not match the way we treat them and the responsibility we allow them to have, in time, we are training them to play in the dirt.

For Christians, playing in the dirt is falling back into the sinful nature. Rather than enjoying the responsibility and significance we have in Christ Jesus, feelings of not being valued begin to rule our minds and hearts. We feel like we just do not matter. We start to entertain ourselves with fleshly things. Our sins don't seem to matter because they make no difference in the lives of the community. We don't feel like others care. We are just regulated to the outfield with all the others who don't matter much. We go from living life to enduring it.

There are two common ways to handle this dilemma. One is the negative way. We can keep yelling at people to quit playing in the dirt. Shame is a tool often used to modify behavior, but it also tends to cause people to hide their faults. Once hidden, these failures avoid discovery and thus avoid maturity and growth. Shame is seldom more than a momentary "fix" if a fix at all. Another strategy is the positive way. Rotate the players into significant positions. Sooner or later everyone will play in the outfield, but that must not be our sole identity. It's not just the good players that matter. Every kid on the team must matter. Because everyone matters, everyone gets an opportunity to be in the infield. Both developing players and discipleship involve the risk of active involvement and significant responsibilities.

As a follower of Jesus Christ, do you feel like your secret sin matters, does it affect the life of the church and the people of God? Do you believe that what you do is related and connected with the lives of others? Or do you feel your life is just in the outfield, on the fringes? If you can do good – great. If not, so what, it really doesn't matter that much. We are all on the same team. We need to stay out of the dirt for both your sake and ours. I had an experience like that while coaching.

One year, I had a child who was down in the dirt all the time. He would take the dirt around the bases and build little pyramids on them. He used his glove more like a backhoe than a baseball glove. Even when he played the pitcher's position, the position that tends to have the most opportunity to field the ball, he would be stacking, smashing and kicking dirt. Then in one game while playing infield, he got his hand stepped on three times. Each of these times, he was stacking dirt on the base when a base runner went by. Since the boys wear rubber cleats, the damage was more than smooth shoes but less then metal spikes. All three times, he "teared" up. When he got to the dugout I asked him, why he was crying. He told me it was because he got his hand stepped on. I asked him if there was anything he could do about that. He didn't answer. Never again that season did I see him playing in the dirt. I think it hurt too much.

Sometimes pain and suffering can actually be a great teacher. We all need to be aware of how much our dirt playing is hurting ourselves and others. Maybe that understanding will come through a broken relationship or through personal suffering. Maybe grace will step on our hand so that we can arise and play on a higher level. "Being in the world, but not of the world" is a lot like being on the dirt but not in the dirt.

It was at the very end of the season, and I was playing my reformed dirt player at the pitcher position. All of the kids had continued to improve throughout the season. They hit the ball harder, ran with more confidence, and were more at ease with the pace of the game. This was a close game and a few of the players wanted me to let the best players take positions in the infield, but it wasn't their turn. We went with who was scheduled. In the final inning, two sharp hits were snagged by our pitcher and easily tossed out at first. As he smiled over his success, I knew that he understood the emotion of being a part of the team. He enjoyed being valued. He had risen out of the dirt, and found new joy on a higher level.

15 Swimming

You are seven years old, and it is summer time. The hot weather, the call of the high dive and the chance to splash water on people and not be punished is too much. You've just got to go swimming. The trouble is that swimming for a few hours in the afternoon results in struggling to stand up and stay awake during the evening game. Swimming zaps your strength and focus, and I understand why many coaches make "no swimming on game days" a rule. The trouble is that the rule "no swimming on game days" is often broken.

A few years back, I had three boys on the team who lived for baseball. The other twelve boys just lived. Over and over again we would have one or two kids who spent the day in the pool and during the game drag their feet on the field. So that year, I often had tension between those who cared only about baseball, and those who cared for other things, too. Judgments, accusations and a few times, bullying took place on our team. For some, "team" meant the most important thing they did. For others, "team" meant one of the many things they did. The ongoing reality was that the behavior of some on the team was directly in opposition to the goals of others on our team. Were we a divided team, compromised? Or were we a team learning to deal with the reality that competing agendas are a part of life?

If you are like I am, and have been around church life for a while, you have most likely encountered the "this is critical" syndrome. One week or one year it is "critical" to read the Bible. The next year or week it may be "critical" to witness or to help the poor. In some spiritual communities, it seems like each week is a lesson on what they need to be totally devoted to that week. Each week the "top priority" changes, and we must re-commit and re-enlist. The Bible has a number of "one things, this one thing I do. (Ps. 27:4; Ecc. 7:18; Mk. 10:21; Lk. 18:22; Phil. 3:13) If the Bible has competing agendas, what should we learn from that? What's the takeaway here? A conflict is often a call to look closer.

That summer, I told everyone on the team that they were free to do and live as they and their families wanted to live. Each one of them was just as important as the others, and each one of them had to choose what he wanted to do. We also talked about how their actions would also affect others. Simply put, I asked them "How do you think you make others feel when you come to a game too tired to play?" "How would you feel if you wanted to win a game and others were too tired to try?" "How do you feel about missing a swimming party when your friends and family are going?"

In the end, we did not solve the problem of swimming on game days. We just came to understand one another and accept the fact that each person has different passions and desires. The result of that conversation was that we even had players volunteer to sit out an inning because they were too tired and did not want to hurt the team. The bullying stopped and so did most of the judgments.

Is it evil or compromising to live as though the body of Christ (your team) is made up of many parts, many passions? Are you an evil person, or do you lack commitment if you don't sell out for this week's directive? Can you have passion for your part and grace for others who equally want to do their part, a different part? It is true that our behavior affects the lives of others. It is also true that we are not called to be jerks, to selfishly live our lives. But most of the time, if we try to build a team as though that team is more important than the whole body, we will be building in a manner different than God builds. God builds in such a way as to require us to relate one to another. If the rules or some agenda is the driving factor, or if the end result is the most important thing, the relational aspects of loving God and loving others will be lost. Achieving the results we want will become the foundation for justifying abuse of others. As we mature in Christ, we don't simply tolerate those who are different; we love them. If we keep on maturing, we will one day find ourselves united with those we once thought most dividing. It's the law of diversity. To become what we are not, we need what we don't have, which at first is what we tend to not like.

16 The Uniform Doesn't Fit

Uniforms in baseball are a big deal. They heighten the emotions of the team. Uniforms are a wearable billboard that says, "I belong." In most coach pitch baseball leagues, the teams have uniforms or team shirts ordered with the names of sponsors and teams on them. While league leaders do their best to provide uniforms, it is impossible to know the shape and size of each player. Later on, players are required to invest more in uniforms, and when the players invest, they tend to get uniforms that fit better. Every now and then I get a player on a team who is larger than our largest uniform or smaller then our smallest uniform. I hate it when that happens.

Those children who are on the extremes tend to be very aware of how they fit into, or fail to fit into, their uniform. When Mom is required to tie a knot in the back of the shirt, or when cotton is stretched like spandex, those wearing the uniforms feel awkward. When this happens, we have taken those children who are the most sensitive to their size and made them stick out. It is amazing how many children actually try to "deal with it." They know they look bad. They know that they are going to look bad all season long. When we fail to cover people properly, we are condemning them to a season of shame or at least embarrassment.

In spiritual life, we can do the same thing. We can have ministries or leaders that allow us to wear an assignment that simply does not fit us. We can focus on "one size" and expect everyone to fit into what we are doing. Having only "one size" tends to lead to deception or outright lying. We want people on our team, so we tell them they look O.K., when they do not. When we place people into what we have available and fail to make available what will fit them, we pass out our team shirts and ask them to "just deal with it." We can also fail to be honest and pretend that the ministry assignment they are wearing, fits. It is not mean to be honest with someone, or honest with ourselves. Our honesty simply needs as much love as truth. If we are not honest, those who publically serve in an area that does not fit them will be exposed to embarrassment. They may play along simply because they long to be a part and to fit in. But in their inner man, they will be enduring an ongoing battle of shame.

I am all for maturity, discipleship and development. But I am against a "one size fits all" living that results in others being constantly exposed. Recent reality TV shows reveal to us that many people who think they can sing, cannot. Many people who think they can teach, lead, or play need to have an honest, loving conversation. They should not be made to live in a spiritual community that tolerates their performance and praises them to their face only to mock and ridicule them behind their backs. People who say, "that was wonderful" to their faces but later criticize and speak honestly about the performance later, are not just two-faced, they are allowing that person to live in shame. It needs to stop. Pretending that "all is great" is different than being open to different levels of ability. Being open to different ability levels is welcoming, pretending that everyone is great, is destructive.

For the uniform that does not fit, a trip to the sporting goods store can often produce a close match. A uniform that is different in style is less offensive than the difference in size. When acquiring a new uniform, buy better quality or style than the original; it will be a way of saying, "I got you covered." In the same way, we need to take time with God's children, and get for them what they need. We may need to be more personal in our discipleship and training. We may need to make places of service and not just offer our traditional spots. We may need to commit more to honesty and actually help others and not just seek for the quickest way to get on with the game.

17 This Is What I am Good At!

It was one of those warm, beginning days of summer. It was our first practice on the field where we played our games, so excitement was high. We had a fence, manicured field and dugouts with seats. It was much better than the backstop stuck out in a grass field where we usually met. We also had a few new players join the roster. I looked up to see a young man approaching me in full uniform. This was only a practice, but his hat, pants, socks and bag all matched. His mom was carrying his bag along with his younger sister, and Mr. T was un-wrapping his brand new baseball bat. As we met on the field and had our first conversation, I was informed by our new player of all the things that he could do. He could run and catch, he could play the field, but what he did the best and what he liked the most, was batting.

I grabbed a ball from that bag and we walked over to start playing catch. I was impressed with all the new stuff he had on. He showed me his new shoes and socks. He told me about just picking out his bag and bat. He showed me the glove he had from last year, but it was just like new. As we lined up about ten feet from one another, I tossed him the ball. He stuck out his arm to defend himself from the toss and jumped to the side as if we were playing dodge ball. It was then and there I realized that Mr. T was doing everything he could to fit into the team because he was afraid of not fitting in based on his ability to play. The long discourse which he used to inform me of all his talents was his way of positioning himself to be accepted.

We live in a modern world where many of us believe we can perform and fit in as long as we can talk about it. Talking, knowing the language, making verbal comments is seen as "doing" in our culture. This is also true in the church world. If we can talk about evangelism, about prayer, about living a holy life, then we are "doing it." We tend to quickly learn the language of the church or gathering so that we can talk to one another and fit in. We don't realize how much pressure a group puts on a person to conform, to fit in. If we neglect and overlook others who are not like us and who fail to use our terms of passion, we are pressuring them with our inattention. People want to belong, so they will talk as though they do. People long to belong, to be a part, to have a place, a team, a family.

Mr. T was devastated when he was publically exposed. It was his first turn at batting practice, and 14 other kids were waiting in the field for him to hit the ball and give them something to do. When swing after swing failed to produce a hit, this young man who boasted in his hitting had to deal with reality. He was at the place where he would go either deeper into deception, or move toward the truth and begin to accept himself and his abilities, or lack thereof. He realized that what he said did not match what he could actually do. He was filled with shame. He had to make a choice. That choice would be affected by our relationship, by how safe or how secure he felt being who he truly was in our presence. On this day, Mr. T stepped toward freedom and enjoyment of the summer of playing baseball with a public proclamation of, "I suck."

This truthful statement was followed by cries of "you can do it" or "swing hard" or "relax and look at the ball" from the other players on the field. Sure, some made comments on his inability, but he was on our team and in time everyone wanted Mr. T to do well because that would help us all do well. That day, a seven year old boy learned that talk is not only cheap, but destructive, if it is not real. Lying to fit in sucks! The pressure to be accepted should not be the cause of our lying or vain boasting. Convincing others that we are better than we are by the use of words is destructive and leads to being judged, rejected and isolated from those we seek to join. Swagger may be all we need to walk the streets, but if we are going to get into the game, we must leave our swagger behind. Joining in to learn and grow is more fun than pretending.

18 Umpires Can Be Intimidated

Rookie baseball is an entry level baseball league. Players who are just learning the game are given an opportunity to play and learn. It is also the entry level for umpires. Men and women, boys and girls who are just starting out as umpires, start in this league; for the most part they too are rookies.

From time to time you run into a coach who can be best described as "aggressive." These are nice men and women who have a deep love for the game and a passion to play. They also have a spirit that strongly desires to win and come out above the opponent. Some tend to speak down to others who are not as aggressive as they are or who may disagree with them.

As you read this, you may think I am being cynical, but that is not my objective. There are people in this world who simply posture themselves as better than others, and we must live at peace with them and with the fruit of their lives. In this case, we must live with their ability to intimidate umpires.

Here is an example. It was a close game and both excitement and tension were in the air. The game had some calls that could have gone either way. The coach on the other team made each one of these a big deal. By "big deal" I mean he let the umpire know he did not like the call. Cries like "O come on now" or "what was that" or "are you kidding me" were proclaimed across the field so that everyone could know that the decision that was just made was not only questionable, but most likely wrong.

After you coach for a while, you can start to see when someone is "working" the umpire. You start to notice the umpire's glances to see if the intimidator desires a certain call. You notice that the umpire is seeking approval from the most verbal or demonstrative coach. You notice how he begins to respond to the side that is making him feel the most awkward. So what do you do? Do you get in there and co-intimidate to work things out so you have a just and equal decision?

Maybe you go the other way and play the good guy. You go to the umpire and show him how kind and understanding you are so that he likes you more than "Mr. Mean." You seek to manipulate, but just from another perspective. After all, it is just a game and getting the call and having your team win is just a part of a game.

Intimidating others has reached new levels in the American culture. Advertising, marketing, sales and even education are all practicing forms of intimidation and manipulation. From power handshakes, to manipulative pleas for us to learn new truths so that we are happier or healthier are a part of everyday life. If you can intimidate a client or co-worker so that you are in a more powerful position or in control, you are seen as just doing what it takes to get the job done or to be successful. Doing what it takes is just a part of living. Intimidation is not bad or evil. There is no moral judgment about it. It is a natural way of life; it is what it is… Or so we think.

With this culture of control, it is hard to teach on the baseball field or in the church the culture of honor, respect, love and kindness. When who we are is so dependent upon a result, when our values or security is dependent upon a fixed outcome, then we must do whatever it takes to achieve that outcome. So, that is why I feel so strongly about helping young children learn a way of life that does not need intimidation for happiness and worth, value or significance.

So, onward with the story. Robert is on third base and takes off for home in a close game. If he scores, we tie it up. If he is out, we lose. The play is close, but Robert is clearly safe, but the intimidation of the opposing coach has worked its magic. With the needful glance of approval, the rookie umpire looks for approval and acceptance. He hears and sees from the opposing coach what is needed for him to be valued, to be approved. The player must be out! The call is made. For this rookie umpire, it is easier to make a bad call than to deal with the external conflict, judgment, public shame or attacks. As a coach what do you do? Do you attack back or build a different kind of culture.

For the player Robert, his value and honor have very little to do with his performance at any given moment. Robert is allowed to make mistakes and to achieve. Robert is a person whom we value because he is a person, not just based on his ability to play, to be safe, and to win a game for us. The right call does not lesson Robert's value or worth. If there is injustice, if Robert is wrongfully accused, if Robert suffers injustice, there is no need to attack. Sure there is freedom to seek to right the wrong. But the same honor we desire Robert be treated with, is the same honor we treat the other coach and the umpire. Evil cannot drive out evil, and intimidation cannot drive our intimidation. It's a culture where how you treat people is far more important than achieving results. Don't worry; great results can come from those who honor others. Just ask Jesus.

So ask yourself, do you want to be a person who values others based on outcome? Do you want to be the kind of Christian who changes the fruit of the Spirit into the fruit of production? Think deeply about it, do you want value to be tied to production? Our modern American culture is rapidly devaluing the elderly, the uneducated, and the unproductive. I once had a spiritual leader who kept saying, "If you're not the lead dog, the scene never changes." He was quite set on being the lead dog and thought his view of things was not only right, but Godly. He was also alarmed and bewildered when those who he had trained in ministry turned on him and attacked him in an attempt to become the lead dog.

71

Our team is sitting on the bench for our post game debriefing. We have just lost a game because of a bad call. The other team is rejoicing in their win. They are even calling themselves champions. Our team is mad, hurt and fighting back some tears as the feelings of failure and worthlessness want to sweep over us. The conversation goes like this.

Coach "What just happened"

Team "We lost," "We got robbed."

Coach "Yep."

And then was the opportunity to be in this world but not of it. "Are we good only if we win..?" "If we lose unjustly, are we losers?" We can regret the loss and yet be joy filled people. We don't need to use intimidation to get what we feel is right. Justifying how we act based on the results we want is not the life we want and certainly not the life God wants for us. The last week of the life of Jesus shows us that we can trust in God even when evil things are being done to us. Injustice does not always win. Even in the face of defeat, real victory is often there, simply hidden from view for a moment or two. It's OK to hurt when we lose, that's a part of competition. It's also OK that when we lose it doesn't ruin our day or cause us to feel worthless. Maybe if I learn that life is still going to be good even if I lose some, I'll seek to manipulate and control others a little less.

19 Failures

A young Mr. K arrives on the ball field. He has no glove and is wearing dress shoes. Dad makes the introductions and begins to shed light on his son's need to be a part of something, to be on a team. Since the goal is being on a team, learning to play baseball was optional. Having a glove and wearing the right clothing are not perceived as important. Mr. K feels no pressure to learn how to play the game. He is not bothered by failure; in fact, his whole goal is simply to be a part. I know it seems crazy, but it happens, and it has happened more than once.

The conflict comes when others strongly desire for him to perform at a certain level, or at least try. When someone is a part of the team and they have no interest in playing or improving, we wonder "why are you here?" There is a temptation to discourage this child from showing up. You are tempted to let the other kids have their way with him and shame him into quitting. After all this is a baseball league, and if you don't want to play the game, if all you want is a place to meet with friends, go somewhere else.

So Mr. K comes. He spends most of his time talking to the other players and distracting them from practice and the game. He is kind and loving and annoying and persistent. He takes his turn at everything and shows no interest in improving. He is content to talk and talk and talk with the others. He is free to share with the coach how little he is actually trying and how he is going to sit and talk to Tim once he is done with his turn at batting practice. Since every player bats in our league, his conversations and friendship times are often interrupted with duties of batting or playing the field. Mr. K is at the ball field, but he is an utter failure at playing ball. It just doesn't matter to him.

Failures are disappointments, mistakes and letdowns. A Failure is something that comes apart, does not work or perform properly; today a failure is something that just doesn't fit in. In youth baseball a failure is not about success, it is about trying, effort. When no effort or desire seems to be present to succeed, it's a mess. Part of being a rookie baseball team is living with and understanding the reality that it is not all about baseball but about 6-9 year olds. The team is about people more than it is about baseball. I don't want it to be, but it is. Youth baseball is about the youth, and they come in all shapes and sizes, intentions and dreams. Not understanding that people matter more than programs can lead to a long season.

If a church is more about mission than about the people, you will quickly find that it is a very unfriendly place unless you are performing in such a way as to help the organization fulfill its mission. The command to go and make disciples of all nations can become a call to focus on programs and measurable goals and avoid difficult people. We can even find ourselves justifying being unkind, unfriendly, unloving to people who will not get with the program. Should we welcome people who are negative, distractive, not serious and not even trying to perform to our standards? Do we love and care for those who are not helping? Did Jesus care for His three best disciples? Did He love the worst one?

It may not seem right that a whole baseball team must suffer the consequences of having a player that is a total failure at playing ball, a person who is not trying. But in reality dealing with failures is a part of life, an everyday part of life. People who disappoint us, make mistakes and let us down are normal. Loving and caring for people who have a vastly different purpose for being on our team is normal. A part of life is understanding others who have no desire to join us in our passion. You can often find a million reasons to cut someone from the team. But can you find one reason to keep them?

Young Mr. K had to deal with a lot of rejection and verbal banter that year, both from players and parents. Mr. K had to listen to cutting remarks and belittling statements as well as outbursts of anger and disgust. Yet, his need to be a part kept him coming back all year. He taught me about insiders and outsiders. He taught me about team and membership. He gave me insight into God's kindness and patience as I "don't even try," or "just attend for friendship," or "don't care about the mission because I just need someone to talk to." If God kicked failures off the team, He would have a very small team. Maybe the Kingdom of God is the only place to come where "being a part" is the only desire. Maybe God is the only coach posting a sign, "failures welcome."

20 The Game of Life

When I was a kid, we had the Milton Bradley game "Life." I can still recall playing this game with my family, laughing about buying kids or picking a low paying vocation. We also purchased the breakfast cereal "Life", and would look and giggle at one another in church when the pastor proclaimed that you cannot buy life. For us "life" was a game, a cereal, and it was, you know – life.

Since that time in my childhood, I have learned, over and over again, that life is not just a game, but you can enjoy living. I have also learned that while you cannot buy life, you can spend your life in great ways. Baseball is one way I have enjoyed spending my life. Playing with my own kids and now with hundreds of others is a fun way to live. There are different aspects to life and to games. First of all, there are, "winners and losers." Secondly, there are emotional highs and lows that come from "winning and losing." And there are questions about what you are purchasing with your life. What are you spending your life on?

Wrestling is also an interesting sport. I don't recall my first wrestling match; it was actually some time before I was ever born. My twin brother and I often engaged in some kind of physical struggle: that's what Mom said. By the time fourth-grade came around, I was an experienced, albeit, an un-coached wrestler headed for the world of amateur athletics. All my life, there has been a winner and a loser. All my life, competition has been a part of my existence. All my life, love and brotherhood have been there, too.

From my experience, I have developed the concept that winning and losing are not bad. The issues of identity, security, competition and rejection have been with me since before I was born. I have won, and I have lost. I have competed to be valued over another, and I have been rejected when someone has been chosen over me. For that first part of my life all that competition, rejection, winning and losing occurred in the context of dealing with my twin brother. In fact, that person was me in a sense because we are identical twins, two kids from the same seed. I love the guy who beat me as much as I love myself, for he is my twin brother. For me, the presence of competition with its winners and losers is defined, not by the winning or losing but by the presence of love. I loved my twin brother, and he loved me, win, lose or draw.

Therefore, I believe that winning and losing are not the big issues; love is. Most people tend to dole out love to winners and not so much to losers.   It's not that keeping score is bad, but loving according to performance is. I like keeping score. Most kids who play baseball want a scoreboard. We like the challenge of winning. That challenge should not be negated because our society has a "love performance" issue. Deal with the real issue of love and breakout the scoreboard.

Dealing with the issues of winning and losing are opportunities to deal with real life. If we are alive, we are going to win, and we are going to lose, so we need to learn to deal with that fact. The child who cannot lose to his siblings at home playing a board game will also struggle on the baseball field. Feelings of failure, rejection, and worthlessness can emerge. In truth, these feelings will emerge unless the child is raised in an environment of deception. No child is the greatest, fastest, or the best at everything. No child avoids faults, failures or the opinions of others. There are reactions to winning and losing. Emotions from boasting, swagger, isolation, rejection and fear are all a part of winning and losing. Add to all these emotions a healthy dose of true love, and maturity can develop. In regard to our emotions, we need to keep adding love.

The next aspect is "what we are purchasing with our lives." As we mature, we begin to live less for ourselves and more for God and others. We start spending our lives for others. Our first step in maturing is usually a desire to be good or do the right thing; in time we learn to love and to give away our lives. The result is that selfishness is replaced with sacrifice; self-interest is lost in honoring others, and we find more joy and happiness than in all of our old selfish pursuits. Finding happiness, and the joy of serving God and others awakens us to the concept of enjoying life. The Bible is true. Giving our lives away is the very best way to find life.

Life is not a game, but it surely seems like one. Winning and losing, being chosen and being rejected, feeling the joy of being in the lead and enduring the pain of coming in last, are all a part of daily life. The mountain tops and the valleys confirm that we are living. The presence of love confirms how well we are living. As a group of children take the field for a season of baseball, becoming a team is basic discipleship. They will be given opportunity to choose to value love over winning and losing. They will get to experience both games and real life. Feelings of homeruns and dropped balls will come and go, but the security and identity of being a family, a team, and being loved will endure when other memories are gone.

As I merge church life and baseball, I hope to encourage you to spend your life well. All of us have limited time on earth. Most of us have limited ability and spiritual gifts. I want you and I to spend our time and gifts wisely for God and one another.

21 Seasons

Both life and baseball come in seasons. For example, in our everyday life we have seasons: winter, spring, summer and winter. If we live in certain climates, we might have a wet and dry season, and in our lives, we have childhood, adolescence, young adulthood, and numerous other divisions that we may title as the seasons of our lives.

With each season come the opportunities to learn and discover new things. Each season starts much like the one before it, and each season is full of its unique and special moments. There is a natural blessing worked into life. We "get to end" a previous season of our lives and "start a new one." "Closure," a word I think I first heard a decade ago, has become quite common. We now hear more and more about ending things and moving on. These are blessings in life and in coaching, in starting a new season and in cutting loose the past so that we can have a fresh beginning. For me, spring baseball season is a new beginning of life and living.

With winter ending and the joy of new relationships, fresh air and new opportunities opening, the past years don't count as I have a fresh start. Of course, adjustments can be made using the wisdom gained, but history is behind me now, and my best planning occurs with a fresh vision and growing hope. It is important to allow yourself the time and energy to develop hopes and dreams. Few of us will enjoy a summer of coaching or playing that is based on "making it" through the season. The worst teams last year can dream of championships. Those teams that find themselves consistently in the middle of the pack can dream of home runs, improved skills and enjoyable outings.

While winning counts, it doesn't need to be the only thing that counts. There is a "law of the middle" that reveals that when we take those middle players out of the mixture and focus only on the best or the worst, splinterization occurs and the "worst" fall further off, and the "best" show little improvement. In academics, military endeavors, and baseball, having a middle group binds the other groups together. This is true for teams and true for leagues. If the teams in the league fail to understand what makes up a league, then teams can find themselves isolated and rejected, hopeless unless they are number one. If a coach understands that those who are "average" are essential to the development of the team, then a team can mature and enjoy "unity."

Here is my list of a mini-season:

- A time to come together
- A time to learn and work with one another
- A time to win
- A time to lose
- A time to endure
- A time to end

Understanding each of these seasons helps build relationships and reasonable goals. Take time to come together, and don't assume that friendship and trust occur just because we all wear the same colors and sit on the same bench. It is important that we help the kids with a "rocket arm" understand how to throw to the timid child, and how the child with emotional outburst can connect with the shy player.

One year I had a child who had been bullied and physically assaulted at school by some children not of his race. When he got to our practices, he saw boys of his attacker's ethnic group. While we can assume that baseball season is all about baseball, it is not. Our baseball season now had the need for a mini-season or a season within a season. We needed to deal with blame, forgiveness, judgments and respect. Pretending that issues were not present was not going to help the boys or the team. Neglecting to deal head on with the issues would only allow room for assumption and false judgments. Who knew youth baseball got so involved.

Churches also need seasons. It would be great to have fresh vision and new players at the beginning of the New Year. Typically, churches do not have any set time to start a new season. This year is governed by what we did last year and a cycle of "doing what we did" is established. Church life tends to be one endless cycle with the past tagging along. To break away from the past, many people leave churches or change ministries. This is one way they can escape the agonizing pressure of never having a new season. Without "new seasons," the people who oversee the evangelism team may find themselves carrying the burdens and outcomes of that ministry from year to year to year. In time, this ministry will be conceptualized more by their past than by their present season.

In some places people get stuck in the same position for decades. Rather than enjoying the energy of new friends and fresh dreams, they are required to deal with faithfulness while they observe new-comers and non-committed servants break free to have fellowship, try new opportunities. Many in our time approach the church with a consumer mindset, seeking for ways the organization can meet their needs. Other people give their lives to the organization and should be provided a fresh season of life from time to time. Doing one's duty, while being honorable, is often without the ability to stop and start afresh. Providing seasons in ministry provides a place for spring to break free or for the closure of a long hard winter.

22 Sunflower Seeds

Sunflower seeds have a long history with baseball. They were five packs for a quarter when I started the habit. For over an hour, I could enjoy having something in my mouth to chew on, plus I got to spit! I like to think that sunflower seeds are truly a gift from God, but the ability to eat them without using your hands must be developed.

Brian seemed to have a special interest in eating seeds. I suspect it was because they were forbidden at home, in the car, or at school. Seeds are often forbidden in all those places spitting is looked down on. I would catch Brian watching me dump a handful in my mouth – followed by the rapid fire "crack" and "spew." On a good day shells can fly like spent brass from a Gatling gun. What boy doesn't want to chew and spit like that?

Brian was a two-hander. Needing two hands to consume seeds is of little trouble in the dugout, but when you take your glove off in the field to break into a little salty delight, trouble is waiting. I recall Brian heading into right field, back pocket bulging with seeds and cheeks swollen with his first load firmly in place.

While the ball was never hit to Brian during that inning, I most remember the crowd noise, probably from family members. They would ask, "What is he doing," or, "Brian, pick your glove up," "Brian, stop that," or "Is he choking?"

In baseball and in life there are distractions, and many of these are enjoyable distractions. Brian was playing his position. He was doing his job. Brian was also enjoying one of the traditions and benefits of the game – seeds. Sure, the result was "unpreparedness." In the spiritual life, we are often caught unprepared because we are enjoying some tradition or benefit. We can lose sight of what is happening as we focus on what we are doing, on what we are enjoying. It is easy to lose sight of the whole game as one part, one position, one delight becomes our focus.

Have you ever encountered fights or arguments at church? Church fellowship meals, worship music, proper offering procedure have all been distractions at times. Maybe you know someone who got distracted with fellowship and forgot to help clean, lock up, or follow through on some commitment. Of course, there are always some who can multitask, who can eat seeds, no hands required. But for the most part, people develop skills through years of practice. Like the disciples of Jesus who mature to the point of being active yet not distracted from the Lord, we too can develop and grow. Our ability is seldom without effort and failure. Most of the time, we "learn to do" by doing. Seldom do we already know "how to do."

For the most part, people are not mad at us for being distracted. They do notice when you lay your glove on the ground and stand unprepared for the position you are in. Don't get upset with calls to "pick up your glove," to "pay attention," to "do your part." Brian could have responded with the modern cultural response that, "I can do whatever I want," but I'm glad he didn't. Selfishness is never a good choice in team life.

The game is over and there is half a bag of seeds left in my pocket. I pull Brian aside and walk him through the process of eating without hands. I send the bag home for some practice. It's like the time I asked a group I was training to have a time of enjoyable worship with the Christian music they were the most offended by. With a little practice, our delights can become non-distractions and our distractions, delights. That is just a little something to chew on.

23 Don't Say Anything

Every now and then I have a surprise reach up and slap me on the face. On this one occasion, it was in the form of a child who truly believed he was a better player than everyone else and possible all the others combined. "I'm better than everyone else on our team, don't you think?" That was the comment he expressed the first time we were sitting together on the beach during a game. Down the row boys leaned forward and turned their faces to see what I was going to say.

What I am going to share I have learned over time. I spent most of my life in the, "say something stupid" stage. I'll call that "stage one." Slowly I progressed to stage two and three. I don't always take the high ground, but I'm learning too more and more. I still "say something stupid" even though I know I shouldn't.

In stage one, when a boastful comment was made, I would go to the opposite extreme and start to point out weaknesses. My antidote for pride was to belittle people. I had acquired some skill at belittling people from my own upbringing. It was quite natural to offer a challenge to arrogance. I used the "strike back" approach. I have come to realize that boys don't respond well to "striking back." If I attack them, they will just defend themselves. Arguments and hurtful comments have never helped me coach a boy or build a team. That's what I call "stupid," it just doesn't help.

In stage two, I would try and ask them a counter question. Thinking that I was Socrates and using his method of asking a leading question, I would try to navigate the child into what I considered a better world view. This method only has a chance if the person is looking for a conversation and not a comment. If the child did not want to be distracted, he simply continued on with his thoughts regardless of any comments I might be making. It was like he was saying, "I don't know what you're talking about, but this is what I am talking about." Asking a boy about life while he is engulfed in telling you how well he hits is like screaming at your teen to turn the music down. He just doesn't hear you.

In stage three, I learned just to not answer. When the pressure got too great to respond, I just calmly walked away. I was not trying to make a statement; I was trying to avoid making a statement. I was not trying to reject, but rather put some space between myself and the issue. I have come to learn that boys often just need the two ingredients of time and life, and they will mature. Not every moment needs to be a learning experience, and in most of these cases the truth is soon in coming. I don't need to rush in and help. Giving some space and time gives life a chance to teach, and there are plenty of life lessons. A few will be at home plate with bases loaded.

That day came when everyone wanted Tony to be as good as he boasted. All his talk had built expectation from the other players. As he dribbled a ball back to the pitcher and was easily thrown out at first base, Tony was being challenged about his self-perception. Life was speaking to him – loudly. No joy is found in seeing people fail. Joy is found in seeing people grow in the truth and be free from bondage.

If we are not careful we can develop the habit of rushing in when we are not needed. Life is at work daily to impart wisdom. Many of the problems we may feel pressure to fix will work themselves out. Not every situation is a need for our input. Some daily issues like hair styles, how I look in these clothes and critical comments about others are often better handled by loving silence, NOT "helpful" responses. Our culture has come to the place where we now believe that sharing our opinion is a human right. We may be free to share our opinion but it may not be the right thing or right time. "feeling free to" and actually helping are not always the same things.

I don't know where the "I have a right to share" mindset comes from. Maybe it is because our world is now so full of social media. Maybe it is because we feel others want us to share our opinion. No matter the cause, we simply do not need to respond to every situation. There are many times in many places where not saying anything is best. The very best!

 In church life we often live with two extremes. We tend to not let anything slide or to let it all slide.   We either confront everyone or correct everyone. We address their ideas and actions or we neglect them. How do we know when it is the right time to say something or when it is not? The answer, I believe, is that we do not know.

The best we can do is to try to listen to God. Listening to God requires not talking for a moment as we seek to hear His wisdom and insight. This pause often helps us avoid our first natural or carnal response. This pause can be the space needed to avoid knee jerk reactions. If we err, we ought to choose to err on the side of patience, long suffering, and kindness. If we are pressured to respond when we don't know what to truly say, we should practice that ancient bit of advice and "say nothing." For just as the boastful sayings of others are evident, so are our reactionary self-assured responses. Our confidence that we know what others should do is the twin to the pride others have in their own ability. Just because we might be in a place of authority, like a coach, doesn't mean we are right.

The world is looking for answers. This is true on the rookie ball field and in life. Most of the time those answers are just waiting for us a few hours or days down the pathway of life. Often a good friend and a good coach will simply walk that path with you, not giving into the desire to instruct you in every situation. I have found that by avoiding my desire to respond I have increased my ability to help.

24 Cheating

The sun was shining and a fresh July breeze blew across the infield. We were enjoying a game where everything was going our way, and we had a huge lead. Cheers were plentiful and celebrations continuous. It was one of those moments when everyone was smiling.

In our league, a ball that is not hit out of the infield requires the runner to only take one base. If the ball goes into the outfield, you can keep on running. This rule was set in place so that a game did not consist of ongoing overthrows and missed plays. The intent of the rule is not to limit the excitement of an extra base hit but to limit the number of errors on any one play.

In contrast to our excitement of winning big, the other team was losing big. We had been in their shoes before, so we knew what they were going through. Our whole team knew by experience the pressure to perform, to make an out, to score a run. That pressure is real and tempting. The cheers from parents may sound more like commands, and the desire to make the most of every opportunity can push you too far.

It all started with a ball hit to third. We were playing the field. The ball was bobbled and the runner went to second. Cheers of "way to go" and "that a boy" helped set the stage for what was to follow. Remember you can't advance on an infield hit, but a trend had started. Two, then three, then four balls were hit in the infield and the players were all coached to keep on running. Since we do not usually have this situation occurring in our games, the kids were unskilled in tagging the runner or making a play on an advancing player. Their inability to get an out discouraged them and caused a downward spiral for us and more excitement and celebration for the other team. Momentum had unquestionably swung the other way.

I started to get mad about this situation and the coach that was "cheating." Our league also has a limit of five runs an inning, so I knew that even with this illegal attempt to win, we would still not lose. But then, after the fifth run and my call for our team to line up and shake hands for the end of game ceremony, the other coach flew off the bench and came screaming across the field with the announcement that the five run rule does not count in the last inning. I asked him why we did not get to keep batting in the top of the inning after we had scored five runs. His answer was, "that was not the last inning." By convincing the youthful umpire, his team returned to the dugout to continue their time at bat. In the end, we lost the game. I think they scored fifteen runs or so in that last at bat. I had a team of crying boys who felt emotionally drained. I had to fight anger.

We don't keep an official score book and there are not official league standings, so the wins and the losses are personal, not official. I was personally upset that cheaters can win. Even as I write this, years later, I am still irritated by it. I am equally troubled by the reality that this other coach delighted in winning through cheating. When I confronted him, his response was simply that he was doing what it took to win.

We all have internal rules, mindsets we use to justify or prohibit breaking the rules. We may have one standard for dealing with taxes and another for filling out a resume. We may feel free to cheat on speed limits, banking mistakes in our favor or punching in on the time clock, but not feel so free when people hit our car in the parking lot, short us at the cash registrar or add fees to our cell phone bill. In church life, we also must deal with double standards, favoritism and bending the rules when one side wants to win.

I admit that what I so easily see on the baseball field, I do not so easily see in the church. I often fail to even perceive when I am taking advantage of the rules or breaking them in order to win, to win for God and church. I fail to see how I am affecting others and how demoralizing it is to those who watch what is going on. God also must be broken of heart as we justify what we do with the claim of "getting the win" for God. I think one good way to overcome the temptation to cheat is to remember how it felt when it was done to you. Remembering how a good day went bad might be what I need to avoid a little fudging of the rules.

25 Cleaning Up

The game is over. Everyone is hot, sweaty and looking for a cold drink. Parents are ready to go and often standing behind the dugout with chair packed, little brother or sister in tow, grandparents in need of an air conditioned, car ride home. So, who is going to clean up the water bottles, the packs of sunflower seeds, the gum and candy wrappers and the half dozen gloves, hats and items left behind in the rush?

When I started to coach, I demanded that everyone was to help clean up the dugout and pick up equipment. I was intolerant of those parents who took advantage of the rest of us and took off as soon as they could. I am sure that I was also visibly upset with boys who made a bigger mess while I was trying to clean up the first mess. I believe that I took a few joyful wins and turned them into dreadful memories as I did what I thought was right in getting things cleaned up.

Then one year I had the youngest boy on the team volunteer over and over again to clean up the dugout and put away the equipment for the team. He was also one of the best players on the team. Over and over again, without any prompting, this joyful child would clean up after the team. Out of duty at first, I started helping him. Then in time, I just enjoyed working with this child, and so we did it together without much notice of the extra work. We were simply enjoying cleaning up as an ongoing part of the playing experience. Then a few other kids stuck around to help. They, too, enjoyed the work as they talked, played, celebrated and related to one another. That was the last year I made cleaning up a big deal, and that was the last year I had issues with help in cleaning up.

That was the year a young man taught me that serving others with joy is attractive. Sure, I had a title and position as coach. Sure, I had duties and time commitments that were pressing on me. Yet, the ten to fifteen minutes extra it took to clean up became a continuation of joyful interaction with others. The game was not all that mattered; people mattered and cleaning up after them was another way of connecting and encouraging. Most every year now, without saying anything, as I clean out the dugout and start to pick up the equipment, players, coaches, parents offer to help. We talk as we work and share our experience. It's work, and it is enjoyable.

In the Kingdom of God, there can also be the pressure to have a position of importance and value. Often this means NOT cleaning up or helping others with "hands on" labor. While thousands of small church pastors know the reality of years of opening and closing the church, few make the transition into joy as they work with others. Most do their duty and impatiently wait for it to be over so they can do what they want to do. Worship leaders, singers, musicians and ministers can all develop an attitude that "leading" is what they are valued for, and that serving in practical ways is not what they are called to do. We have become a people who honor people for what they say or sing and fail to know who they truly are. I know by experience that we can teach on serving others for years and never do anything other than what we want to at the same time.

Cleaning up is work, but it is also enjoyable.

26 Not Showing Up

In my first year of coaching coach-pitch baseball, I was focused on winning and having each player perform at his best level. I planned the practices so that we could get the most out of our time and players. With the first few practices the emotion and energy was high; everything was new, so we progressed nicely. Then, slowly, kids started not showing up for practice. I sought to encourage and motivate them by telling them how important it was for the team that each player show up. I told them that working hard at practice would pay off in the games. I tried to find out why more and more kids were laying out of practice and showing up only for the batting cage times.

Later, I had a conversation with one of the parents about the attendance of their child. "He simply doesn't want to come," was not the answer I was expecting. I thought there were competing events, conflicts with the family schedule or some important matter that was drawing the player away from practice. I was not aware of how connected attendance and interest are. I was raised in the age where your commitment determined your attendance, not your interest. I was still living in the world of joining a team means doing all that the team does. That day has long become extinct.

In the community of God the same culture exists. Many of those who follow the Lord passionately today are committed according to interest level. Those who attend the church every time the doors are open, just because the doors are open, are few and far between. We can't expect people to come and participate simply because "this is what we are doing." People vote with their attendance. This is true in our religious gatherings and on the ball field.

Sometime in the 1990s, it was projected that soccer would replace baseball because in soccer more people get to "play." Soccer offers more involvement and allows the players to take an active part, less standing and waiting in the outfield. My goal is not to keep baseball alive, but rather to find a way to bring greater involvement and participation into the game. The goal of involvement is based in the needs of the kids to have fun and be an active part. The players want to play. They don't want to have a few opportunities to run, hit and throw. They want more.

Could it be that church attendance is declining because we are not involving people? Sure, we may be having a great training time, and think we are offering a wonderful time of equipping the saints, but if they are not showing up, something could be wrong. We may be living in the past and disregard the need for significant involvement. We may need to help each person be who they are called to be and focus less on what the organized church needs to survive. I say that because much church training is about ushers, sound technicians, prayer teams, teachers and worship teams. While these are very important jobs, most believers are not called or involved in these areas and therefore have no need to be a part of our training. Even our training to be "a radical Christian" may need some readjustment so that God's people could be equipped to be an everyday believer in this city or in this marketplace.

Toward the end of that first year I started to have more and more practice stations going on at the same time. We would hit using the batting "T", and with the whiffle balls, and with the coach pitching in the field all at the same time. Added to this, we also could be hitting pop flys to the outfield and have a bucket on second base serving as a target for those catching those flys. Interest and attendance increased.

27 Don't Coach Your Son

Terry was playing catch with his dad about twenty minutes before practice the first time I met the two of them. Dad was eager to help and showed a lot of interest in the game. It is essential to have help coaching the team. Multiple coaches allow for more personal instruction, more training, more encouragement and more insight.

I first noticed that something was not right after Terry got a hit and didn't run all the way through first base. He was safe, but his dad coached him on running through. Dad's advice was right and if heeded would pay off. Terry heard what his Dad/Coach was saying, and he took it to heart. But something more was going on. Terry's relationship with his Dad was changing.

In later games, Terry made a couple more mistakes and struck out. His Dad/Coach addressed each issue and offered good advice. The emotions were encouraging and the insight helpful. However, the relationship between father and son kept getting worse and worse. By the end of the third or fourth game, the son didn't want anything to do with his dad. A normally comforting hand on the shoulder was shrugged off like an unwanted weight.

What happened that day has happened again and again over the seasons and has been the cause of me implementing a policy that "Dads can't coach their own sons." Now I know that many fathers seek to coach their son's team for the very purpose of being together. I am for them being together. I am for a father coaching the team on which his son plays. I am just not for the added tension and strain on relationship that can occur when a dad coaches his own son. I ask the dads to let the other coaches coach their son. This allows the dad and son to have a relationship after the game that is based more on their relationship than on performance. From time to time, I have been tempted to get rid of this rule as many dads are great coaches and great encouragers. Then some dad will come along and demand more out of his child than the other kids, or a Dad will "ride" his child, embarrassing and shaming them. So, I keep the policy in place.

Smaller Christian communities can have a lot of shame and embarrassment because the only one to coach the team is also the "father" of the spiritual family. In large church settings, a leader can have someone else intervene in situations that require correction or redirection. I learned this early on in the ministry when I was on staff at a large church and the Senior Pastor had me meet with people and confront situations that needed to be addressed. Later, he would meet with the same people. This separation allowed for the senior leader to have influence while avoiding feelings of shame, failure or insecurity on the part of the congregation.

Terry loved his dad being a coach on the team as long as Terry did well. Whenever he missed a ball or struck out, Terry had to deal with the pressure of his performance and the desire to please his dad. The desire that a child has to please his dad and the dad's desire for his son to play well is just too much for many seven year olds to handle. I believe a buffer is wise.

Later in the same year, Terry lazily ran to first base following a hit. I yelled direction and encouragement at him. Terry took it to heart, and after the game I heard father and son commenting on the event. Dad addressed the issue as Dad and not coach. This allowed both of them to enjoy the game and maintain the relationship that would last them the rest of their lives as father and son. Those of us in the church can learn from this. We need more life coaches to step up and give a buffer to family life, single moms, and spiritually young parents. Over burdening, even the best of us, can lead to strained relationships.

28 Correct Quietly

I grew up in a family that yelled. We played games in the outdoors. We talked over farm equipment, over construction noise and often over each other. I enjoyed yelling to one another as we fished, hunted, hiked and tried to find the truck to go home. Working construction for years and yelling to other workers was normal. Volume was needed over the sound of saws, trucks and other screaming workers. While many still practice the art of yelling, for some it is often associated with anger and not volume. When people raise their voices, it can be interpreted more as rage than as a need to be heard across the field or above the crowd. From time to time, I have had a parent come to the back of the dugout and say, "we don't yell at our children."

It has been hard for me to reel in something that has been a part of my entire life. It is also hard to change a behavior that you don't feel is wrong. To alter the way you are just for others requires you to care and love for others more than you do yourself. It is hard.

I also had to learn boundaries. Yelling out instructions and help to our team seemed to be acceptable. I was still able to loudly declare where to throw the ball or which base to run to. But the more personal corrections were no longer loudly publically voiced. The verbal prompts given from the sideline to the batter at the plate have been replaced with a few quick steps toward the player and a softer direct face to face encounter.

At first, I thought this "new" approach was simply going to be a burden. In time, I learned that it was more personal. A conversation is often heard while a yell is often only listened to. I think I have become a better coach by learning to correct quietly.

In the community of God, correction often becomes public. I believe this happens because there is a need for someone to be right and someone to be seen as wrong so others won't follow in the errant pathway. A leader/coach is seeking to direct the community of God by determining what is right and what is wrong. When it is not a leader, it may be a board, a counselor, or a set of traditions. In the end, we try to make the future easier than the past as we use correction to control. This is normal in the church and on the ball field.

Open correction can be highly emotional. These public personal conversations tend to cause us to experience heightened emotions because others are "listening in." When this happens, the "rules" are much harder to focus on because of our feelings. Public correction tends to be one-sided. Having time to listen to the other person or to understand their motives is lost in the method of correction. I can recall going to a church where the pastor shared from the pulpit during his sermons any rules that were broken or needed to be addressed.   One Sunday the public correction was about people smoking in the parking lot. On another occasion it was about the way communion was served. Both corrections ended with his declaration of "this is the way we do it here."

As a coach, I need to balance control and conversation. Do I have time for a seven year old to share with me his perspective? Can I see beyond winning the game? Do I know their perspective on the situation?

One day I had a very special boy on the team who desired to baptize others on the team with Gatorade. When his bottle was empty, he started using any others he could find. Those being immersed did not enjoy the act even though it was quite hot that day. I wanted to verbally blast this boy. I did not want to have a conversation. I wanted a resolution to the problem, and I wanted it now.

I cannot recall the name of this boy although I can still see him plainly in my mind's eye. As I sat next to him and asked him to put the lid back on the bottle he just picked up I could feel the tension. I know I looked mad because I was. We talked. I then learned that a boy of his age and maturity could actually think that such an act was seen from his perspective as fun and joyful to others. He honestly did not think that others would be mad. He thought it was all good.

When we correct quietly, we often discover that the motives of others are not what we thought they were. It is easier to love and care for people who simply make mistakes. This is true in a Gatorade soaked dugout and in a parking lot with no ash trays.

29 Shortcuts

It was opening day and energy was high. Smiles and hopes exploded from faces. We were sitting on the grass for a group team meeting, and each child was anxious to start. The beginning of the season is the start of competition, and everything seems to be a contest: Who will be the first to sit down, to stand up, to get onto the field, to reach the dugout. As we released twenty some kids, they bolted through a narrow gate and raced to the start of the season. Not everyone would make it though.

Lamont was a natural athlete. During the pre-season practices, he had shown us that he knew how to play ball, how to run and how to have fun. He was not the kind of kid who would come in last at anything. That day, however, would be different.

The group was released; the gate onto the field filled up, and Lamont decided to take a shortcut. One hand on the top of the fence, one foot placed halfway up, one lunging swing and he was topping the fence. As he was almost over, he caught his toe, his weight shifted and the mass of his body landed on his wrist. Tears filled his eyes. His wrist was broken.

Lamont came up with a plan to beat the rest. He was going to take a shortcut. Often shortcuts seem like the solution. A moment of risk and a lasting reward is what seems to be promised. As we get older, we have experienced some of the disappointments of shortcuts, and we often know that they are not as appealing as they appear. Shortcuts can cost us! Lamont had to pay full price for his shortcut. It cost him the race, the opening game and the season of baseball. A decision to "get ahead" put him behind.

In life, I have seen a lot of shortcuts and have taken a few myself. I believe that I even got away with a few, but I have come to learn that some of those I thought I got away with have actually had lingering results. There are times when we fall and know right away that we are hurt. At other times, we don't realize that we have sustained an injury until years later. Shortcuts are not the same as being productive or efficient. Shortcuts are ways we leave the path, avoid the gateways and try to reach a destination by creative, but often unacceptable means. They are "overly creative ways" to balance the books, to get down the mountain, to put brakes on cars and to get to the dugout.

Time pressures us to take shortcuts. How long something takes is a way we score winning, and it is a way we determine ability. Do you have time to make that phone call, to double check your answers, to go through the right procedure? Do you have time to communicate to all those involved? Won't they understand that I'm not trying to cheat; I'm simply out of time.

The ways of the world have crept into the Kingdom of God through our ideas and use of time. "Hurry" and "urgent" are so overused they now seem "normal" in most of our minds. When was the last time we encouraged someone to "take their time" and do a good job? Good jobs are done fast, efficiently and within limited time frames. The church once taught that we have enough time to do everything God desires of us. Now we live as though God is only happy if we are pressure driven. Conversations, friendships and fellowship that are not directed toward fulfilling our goals are seen as "bad management." What do we do under this pressure? We take shortcuts.

Here is my list of shortcuts that I wish I could do over.

- Listen carefully to people who disagreed with me.
- Slow down on implementing change and not push it through.
- Put things away where they belong the first time and avoid handling them twice.
- Speak the truth in love and don't use the shortcut of "not the right time" to speak.
- Grab Lamont as he runs past me and onto the fence.

Lamont kept on showing up for games and practice. His heart to play ball was not holding him back; it was his hand. Hours of joy and laughter, running and even swimming were lost as the result of a moment of passion. The call to win the race is only rewarding if we run in accordance to the rules. (1 Cor. 9:25)

30 Absolutely Urgent

I started wrestling around the 4th grade, followed by little league baseball, Jr. High football, track and basketball. I played my way through college and had many good times. I won a fair share of games and matches. But winning was not the end-all for me. Doing my best as a person and doing our best as a team somehow became more critical to me than winning.

Today, I often see winning as the main goal. I have competed against coaches who yell, scream, throw fits of rage, and pout about a game. In truth, however, most of the players simply want to have fun. With one exception, all the boys I have coached so far came out to play baseball for one reason, to "have fun."

Winning is important, for it assists in character development and serves as an evaluation tool. Keeping score helps focus and builds into young lives the premise that hard work matters. In the world of sports having fun does not need to be purposeless. It just needs to be fun.

Now I admit that if you want your seven or eight year old to be Mr. Baseball, I am not the coach for you. I will also tell you that if you want your seven or eight year old to love playing baseball when he is nine through fourteen, I might be the guy you need. I have seen numerous boys stop playing baseball because "it isn't any fun." I have seen boys who are slower to mature physically spend a summer on the bench, discouraged as they watch others play. And skilled boys, pressured to win every game, as if the value of their life depended upon the season, were defeated by the never ending stress to win.

In our churches, I often hear the call to be a radical follower of Jesus. "Radical" is presented as what is needed to accomplish the next goal, to be a winner. Demand after demand is placed upon God's faithful to do more and more and more. If they take a vacation, if they want a break from ministry, if they withhold from giving in our next effort, they are chided and questioned. It may not happen in public, but I have been and heard enough to be sick of it. Pressure is motivational tool number one.

I strongly believe that people who delight themselves in the Lord will out work those who labor under the yoke of performance. I am amazed that the church has kept as many workers as we have. We often require people to serve for years with very little personal encouragement. We throw a workers' banquet and include a statement in the year-end report and think we have treated them well.

It is my observation that revival is also fun! In my experience, working hard with God is fun. Fun, enjoyment and rejoicing are present when we work with God. Delighting ourselves in the Lord is just that, a delight. The yoke of God is easy. So what is this yoke of obligation and performance like?

Stop presenting every issue and every item on our agenda as urgent, absolutely necessary, critical for world transformation and essential for those who love God. We need to honor others and trust them to live lives worthy of the Lord and to enjoy that life. If the Lord is my delight, I will fulfill my duty. As I carry my load for the Lord, I want to have a song in my heart and a smile on my face. Rejoicing in the Lord is my goal, not because I have to, but because I am having fun with the Lord. If there is anything that is absolutely urgent, it is delighting in the Lord.

31 Wiffle Ball

I have coached for several years and experienced some teams that loved practice and others that seemed to hate it. Year by year each group of boys is different. Desiring to get the most out of each practice, I know that interest matters. When the kids put forth effort, they learn, develop and mature as ball players. When they are just going through the motions, we spend more time chasing the ball than catching it. And then one year, another coach told me to have wiffle ball games.

Taking his advice, I set up a wiffle ball field for some practices. The bases were brought in close, and a homerun fence set in place. Gloves were tossed aside, and we moved to an all grass area so that sliding and diving would be easier. We were going to play by all the normal baseball rules. Excitement soared, interest and focus were in vast supply, and homeruns became the source of smiles and swagger.

Fun and success encourage hard work and effort. A passion for playing is passed on as children delight in what they are doing. When hitting a homerun is doable, every batter has focus. When the ball is plastic, few feel it will hurt when it hits them. When the bases are short, even the slowest runner hustles to beat out the throw. Parents celebrate, and the coach delights to see the effort. Wiffle ball is a win, win, win.

Is there a place to play wiffle ball in church or the Kingdom of God? Is there a place to enjoy practicing? With all the eternal consequences, is there any time to be rejuvenated and enthused about living a life of surrender and sacrifice? I think there is. Pushing aside the pressure to always be serious, we can find that fun and joy aid in our development of holiness. The pressure for church to be a production can be reduced and the renewal of spiritual life can be infused in others as we delight in the Lord, in others and in ourselves.

At the heart of baseball practice and church life is the question, "what is required of us?" Does a good practice require straight lines, little talking, endless hustling and tight time scheduling? Can we enjoy what we are doing and not negate the eternal consequences, the importance or the ability to truly develop? In the end I hope we see that not all practices are a wiffle ball game, but some are. Not all we do in the body of Christ is for fun, but some is. The abundant life of Jesus may involve some seasons of great sacrifice and some of celebration. Like a wedding feast or a baseball season, there will be a mixture of serious and fun, resulting in some serious fun.

32 Sharing

A young man enters the dugout with a new helmet or bat. He is beaming. He wants to stand out, to show off his new stuff, to be valued and possibly envied by the others. Then he finds himself surrounded by those who want to use his bat or helmet. To his surprise, and often to the horror of the parents, someone uses the bat or helmet without permission. At this age being allowed to use someone else's stuff is a "like." Not being allowed to borrow is a "dislike." Then the very best/worst thing happens. This young man heads to the plate only to discover that his helmet is on the head of the runner on second.

Sharing is more than a rule; it is also an art and a painful lesson in sacrifice. I have heard little boys say, "It's mine, my dad bought it for ME!" I have heard the same thing in the church. People yelling at others about what Father God has given to them. Screaming for others to get their hands off what they believe is their ministry, their microphone, their program. "Father God gave this to me, and this is what makes me special, me important, me valued,"

Over the years I have made the rule, "Don't bring it if you don't want to share it." There is enough drama and pressure on kids, and I don't need to open the door for some to be favored and others to be neglected. In the past, I allowed the kids to just work it out, but the child with the "good stuff" used it to buy friends or earn favors or sunflower seeds. Limited sharing sowed the seeds of limited team. Some were together, others were left out and punished publically with a loud, "That's mine; get your hands off it." It has even gone so far as to resound with, "my dad said that you can't touch it, and if you do he is going to …."

In church, we also have places or services that tend to end up as stations of ownership. The sound system, the seating, the communion ware; all become things to be owned, controlled. We tend to share with our friends but struggle to have all things in common.

In the middle of a baseball season, I sometimes need to start over with our sharing policy. Often I need to restart, re-launch. In the body of Christ, we may need to have a start over also. We need to use what we have to build and help others, not to control or rule our special area. Sharing with those we like and neglecting others is such an epidemic in the body of Christ right now that we don't even see how sick it is. In both the church and the ball field, we think it is proper for people to withhold common items of community use. From toys in the nursery to kitchen items, from teaching supplies to microphones, "mine" often overrules "ours."

It is sad, but it must be said, sharing has fallen so far off the normal Christian life, that the people of God justify apathy and sloth by claims that "it isn't my responsibility." We don't share in the cleaning, the serving, the maintenance, and in the unseen and seldom honored places in the Kingdom of God. It's not my job to help in the parking lot, to pick up after the fellowship, to clean the dugout after the game. Such is the world of not sharing.

You can get the "evil eye" for repositioning chairs or rearranging the bulletins; you may be escorted out of the kitchen or off the stage if you don't honor the "personal rights" of someone. We often fail to see that what we are actually "touching" is another's identity or control. We are not just using their microphone; we are using their identity, value and significance.

When it is your turn at bat and nine out of the last twelve kids just sweated in, dropped in the dirt, and accidently slobbered on your new helmet; sometimes the old helmet looks a lot better. Common use doesn't have to mean common abuse, but it tends always to mean common value, or shared.

33 More on Rules

I know that I have already shared on rules earlier in this book. This section is much like the last, with a little difference that might connect with others dealing with the life of rules and the life of justice.

I had a brilliant young man once who greatly desired to bat and who did not like playing in the outfield. Over and over again, he started to overheat, or needed to go to the bathroom or needed to get his water from his mom when it was time to play the outfield. Yet, I noticed that this did not happen when he was playing the infield. I was tempted to make the rule: if you don't play the outfield, you don't bat. That would appear to solve the problem, but I was making a rule to control one boy. What if that rule, made for that boy, hurt another player who didn't have the negative behavior but just got caught in the circumstances. Should the boy who on occasion truly needed to use the bathroom, be punished by a rule I made to control another boy's behavior?

Over the years, I have learned that I can manage the team through rules or through relationships. If I choose to coach via rules, then I make a list of behaviors and whenever that behavior is not being followed, I point out and scream out the rule. This method is quicker and easier than relating to people, especially seven and eight year old baseball players.

So, I started making fewer rules and building more relationships. I had to take the time and deal with people. I had to speak honestly about how I felt about their behavior and listen to their responses. I was burdened down not only with the behavior or situations, but with them.

By burdened down, I mean the constant need to relate was heavy, I felt less in control. And then I got it!

I wasn't there to play baseball, I was there for them. The game is what they played, and I was there to serve them so they could do that. Managing the team was more than making sure the game was played right. I was there to manage the boys and to relate, and coach them. My job was to work for them, to serve them.

In the Kingdom of God we often make a rule so that we don't need to develop a relationship. We make long lists of things to do and not to do. Benevolence, ushers, worship leaders and musicians, nursery workers are just a few of the "follow the rules" ministries in most churches. We tend to think that leadership is there to be served (by following the rules) rather than by teaching us how to serve. Equipping people is more than giving them a list of rules. Equipping is supported by relationships. We tend to give out "equipping manuals and materials" that have detailed ways to serve. We tend to give people books and websites and articles, almost anything other than giving them ourselves.

One season I had a boy who kept hitting the other kids in the head with his bat while waiting to bat. The good news was that he waited to hit them until they had their batting helmet on. The bad news was that he refused to stop. I had the rule, no hitting others with the bat. It didn't stop the behavior. I ended up going over and standing by this young boy every time he was on deck. It took about four games of my presence intervening in the hitting to get it to stop. What the rule could not train this young man to do, I could train him to be by being with him. I often wonder if that is the reason that God is with us. Yes, we have the Bible, but God is with us.

34 Correcting With A Smile

At times, I have found myself yelling while standing in a sea of screaming people. To deal with this situation I learned, at an early age, to yell loudly. After all I was a twin, and I needed to be heard above the competition of my brother.

Kevin was a young man who was not raised anything like I was raised. His single mom was a consoling and quiet person. Kevin was tender hearted, and had a great desire to please people. He was the kind of boy who wanted me to be happy, and he often gave a glance my way to see if he was meeting my wishes. He also was not familiar with baseball, and his need for approval often caused a delay in action that cost him embarrassment, and our team an out.

Kevin was playing in the outfield. He was doing his best to stay focused, and I could tell he was longing to kick the dandelions and gaze at the passing butterfly, but for the most part he resisted that urge. A ball was hit at Kevin, not more than ten feet from him. Kevin looked at the other players, looked at me, back at the other players and then finally ran toward the ball.

When I yelled at Kevin, he reacted as though I was shooting a gun at him. For a while, I thought he might not even come into the dugout at the end of the inning. Kevin was not able to hear what I wanted him to hear because he was experiencing a big, loud, excited male. This was something that was overwhelming to Kevin at this time in his life.

In community, we often make the mistake of telling someone the truth without any awareness of their ability to hear. Fear, past experiences, pain, intense longings, all affect a person's ability to hear what we are saying. We make a mistake to think that that fearful person is just dealing with information. Most of the time we are dealing with the culture, the context, and the way that information is being delivered.

In community and in families and on the ball field, we are not coddling or babying people if we understand who they are and what they are going through. If we know how to correct a person without making them deal with a minefield of personal issues, we are acting in wisdom, not over protection. Selfishness needs to do things my way. Love often finds a more helpful way.

Throughout the year, I seldom yelled at Kevin in the field. When he got to the dugout, I would go over to him and sit down, making sure I had a big smile on my face. I learned to ask a question first, getting him to open up and talk before I shared correction. All this may seem like an awful waste of time to get someone to aggressively run after a baseball, especially when there are four of five people waiting on the bench for an opportunity. But that is the point. On the field and in spiritual community, we don't just play to win, we play to help and encourage one another while taking time to smile.

35 Take The Blame

As I look out my window in March, there is snow on the ground. When I drive around town after school, I will not see children out playing and running around, because most of them will be huddled down at home watching TV or playing video games. This means that the baseball season will most likely get a late start, and by the time the first game comes around, players may have had as little as an hour or two of practice. That is what happened a few years back.

It was the third game of the season, and we had had only a handful of hits. The wind still blew cold, and interest in baseball was focused more on how to stay warm than how to swing a bat. Players tried to fit stocking caps under helmets and winter gloves inside gloves. The team knew that we were bad, and everyone who came to watch us knew it, too. I felt worthless about our performance. I wanted to complain, blame and get the parents to think I was a good coach.

In the natural, it may not seem right to take the blame for things that you cannot control. When it comes to a team, to leadership, we need someone to step up from time to time and take the blame. Guilt or innocence is not the issue. What these forward thinking leaders and coaches do is to provide a way for complaining to end and hope to begin.

Jesus took the blame for the sins of the world on the cross. He was not guilty. When he stepped forward and shouldered the cross, He gave all of us a way of hope. Jesus is the Savior of the world, and in life we often need saviors to enter into the events of our lives. However, we are never to have the mindset of being Christ Jesus. We are called to be like Christ, to bear one another's burdens and to do our part.

In church leadership, I often see a failure to take the blame. When things go bad, when our performance is bad or the results despairing, we tend to give a long list of excuses. If a leader stepped forward and took the blame, most institutions would probably fire him. They shouldn't. They should give him a raise. When someone takes the blame, they make a way for others to start again, to be renewed, to discard guilt and shame. Jesus did this for us, and we can do it for one another in small, yet meaningful ways.

In the season that started so badly, we ended up in the middle of the pack. We were not the best team, and we were not the worst. What we did not have was a nagging fear of being worthless game after game. The boys playing the game were free to try, to enjoy. When a coach takes the blame, they remove shame and the haunting voice of belittlement. The same is true in spiritual community. How many organizations would be better if people could just start over? What if you did not need to leave a community to be set free from your past? What if hope was more plentiful than grumbling about past performance?

God will hold us all rightly responsible for every action and thought. Showing mercy through the means of "taking the blame" may not be the worst action to take.

36 Passion Driven

If you have been around youth baseball, then you most likely have experienced a coach that was passion driven. These coaches have a driving passion for all they do on the field and ask that each and every player also have a visible passion. Passion driven coaches seem to have an ample supply of both encouragement and criticism. They tend to get things done by an expression of passion. They see that their team can always do more. They tend to follow every complement with a list of things the boys could do better.

What I think I have observed over the years is that everyone loves a passion driven coach, at first. The excitement, the zeal is welcome to begin the season, to build momentum. As the season rolls along, however, players and parents tend to get tired of never being quite good enough. They tire of the complement that seems to be more manipulative than real, while the list of things to do better is the real focus. Everyone gets tired of unending striving. It is weary to have your best day crowned with a plea to make the next outing even better.

In the spiritual community, I have seen a thousand examples of leaders who drive their people by passion. An endless list of objectives and requirements for the Godly, passionate follower are offered. As soon as one thing is done, two or three more are brought in for regained focus. When people remove themselves from the passion driven lifestyle, even for a short time, they are judged as lukewarm, backsliding (an old term) and uncommitted.

Passion is OK, but wisdom is much better.

I have seen a passion driven coach try to help a player catch the ball. Time and time again the ball is tossed in the air toward the player. "Catch the ball" is resounded over and over and over again as the player seeks to please the coach. When the coach's limit of positive encouragement has reached its max, expressions of "come on now," "try harder," and "you can do it" fill the air. What you seldom hear is how to catch the ball.

Each year, I usually have at least two players who fear being hit by the ball. This makes it very hard for them to catch the ball because they do not want to get anywhere near it. I usually start playing catch with these guys standing about three feet away and without gloves. I ask them to use only one hand and when the ball touches their hand to squeeze their hand shut. My premise is that if you cannot catch the ball with your bare hand, you most likely will not know how to use the glove to catch the ball. In most cases, most young boys will use the glove as a shield.

I must admit that early on as we progressed in this "learning to catch" process, I made some mistakes. One of them occurred over and over again until I figured out the problem with my instructions. As we progressed and had the gloves on, I asked the players to reach toward the ball when it was coming. Reaching toward the ball was my instruction to get them more aggressively going after the ball and not just lifting up their gloves hoping that the ball lands in it. Have you ever played catch with a player who got mad because you could not throw the ball into his glove every time?

As we progressed from tossing the ball back and forth to tossing pop flys, I had several kids lift their gloves into the air toward the ball. When they did this, the ball was often hidden from their line of sight. It seemed like each child waited until as long as they could without seeing the ball, and then they would move their glove out of the way just as the ball was arriving. In this way, I instructed several children how to get hit in the face with the ball. To redeem that situation, I now have them wait as long as possible before reaching toward the ball. Passion did not solve the problem; wisdom did.

How can we act in more wisdom in the spiritual community? How can we stop demanding more and more and more followed by judging one another more and more and more? I believe we can stop believing that the Kingdom of God is advanced by "activity" alone. Doing all the stuff that needs to be done or spending our lives doing good works is not the same as trusting and fully obeying our Father in Heaven. We tend to have a lot of faith that God will bless our works and very little faith that God will tell us what needs to be done. We tend to be in a hurry to get everything done and the result is we have a culture full of passionate religious activity and little transformation.

Without going into a whole ordeal about how to become wise, we can all start by living out the 1 Corinthians 13 passage on love. Being patient, kind, and living out the other expressions of love is living in wisdom. It will include passion. It just won't be driven by it.

Notes

Notes

Notes

Notes

Notes

www.ingramcontent.com/pod-product-compliance
Lightning Source LLC
Chambersburg PA
CBHW020508040426
42331CB00042BA/80